IMAGES

Other interview books from Automatic Press ◆ⱽ⁄ₚ

Formal Philosophy
edited by Vincent F. Hendricks & John Symons November 2005

Masses of Formal Philosophy
edited by Vincent F. Hendricks & John Symons October 2006

Philosophy of Technology: 5 Questions
edited by Jan-Kyrre Berg Olsen & Evan Selinger February 2007

Game Theory: 5 Questions
edited by Vincent F. Hendricks & Pelle Guldborg Hansen April 2007

Philosophy of Mathematics: 5 Questions
edited by Vincent F. Hendricks & Hannes Leitgeb January 2008

Epistemology: 5 Questions
edited by Vincent F. Hendricks & Duncan Pritchard September 2008

Philosophy of Medicine: 5 Questions
edited by J. K. B. O. Friis, P. Rossel & M. S. Norup September 2011

Narrative Theories and Poetics: 5 Questions
edited by Peer F. Bundbaard, Henrik Skov Nielsen & Frederik Stjernfelt 2012

Intellectual History: 5 Questions
edited by Morten Haugaard Jeppesen, Frederik Stjernfelt & Mikkel Thorup May 2013

Philosophical Practice: 5 Questions
edited by Jeanette Bresson Ladegaard Knox & Jan Kyrre Berg Olsen Friis January 2013

The History of Logic in China: 5 Questions
edited by Fenrong Liu & Jeremy Seligman September 2015

Science and Religion: 5 Questions
edited by Gregg D. Caruso March 2014

Peirce: 5 Questions
edited by Francesco Bellucci, Ahti-Veikko Pietarinen & Frederik Stjernfelt July 2014

Social Epistemology: 5 Questions
edited by Duncan Pritchard and Vincent F. Hendricks, January 2015

See all published and forthcoming books in the 5 Questions series at
www.vince-inc.com

IMAGES: 5 QUESTIONS

EDITED BY

AUD SISSEL HOEL

PEER BUNDGAARD

FREDERIK STJERNFELT

Automatic Press ♦ $\frac{V}{I}$ P

Automatic Press ♦ $\frac{V}{I}$ P

Information on this title: www.vince-inc.com

© Automatic Press / VIP 2016

This publication is in copyright. Subject to statuary exception and to the provisions of relevant collective licensing agreements, no reproduction of any part may take place without the written permission of the publisher.

First published 2016

Printed in the United States of America
and the United Kingdom

ISBN-10 / 87-92130-55-0
ISBN-13 / 978-87-92130-55-6

The publisher has no responsibilities for the persistence or accuracy of URLs for external or third party Internet Web sites referred to in this publication and does not guarantee that any content on such Web sites is, or will remain, accurate or appropriate.

Cover design by Vincent F. Hendricks

Contents

Preface	vii
Acknowledgements	ix
1. Mieke Bal	1
2. Gernot Böhme	9
3. Marta Braun	13
4. Horst Bredekamp	17
5. James Robert Brown	21
6. Matthias Bruhn	27
7. James Elkins	37
8. Groupe μ	41
9. Robert Hopkins	49
10. John Hyman	57
11. Claude Imbert	63
12. Martin Jay	71
13. John M. Kennedy	77
14. Dominic McIver Lopes	89
15. Patrick Maynard	95
16. W. J. T. Mitchell	105
17. Bence Nanay	109
18. Barbara Maria Stafford	121
19. Felix Thürlemann	127
20. Kendall L. Walton	135
About the Editors	139
Bibliography	141

Preface

───────────── ♦ ─────────────

The study of images and their use as media for communication, expression, reasoning, persuasion and much more, is a relatively recent development in academia – even if the inquiry into the nature and value of depiction goes back to at least Plato. It has several different roots: in philosophers investigating representation and evidence, in art historians exploring the status of one of their major objects, in structuralists advancing the idea of a visual semiotics, in psychologists experimenting on perception and cognition, in media scholars focusing on the persuasive and ideological powers of images, in historians of science scrutinizing the role of diagrams in the development of the sciences. The study of images is a genuinely interdisciplinary field, and our aim with this book is to provide a snapshot overview of this emerging field of study by means of a special tool developed by the *Five Questions* book series. The tool is to conduct a series of targeted interviews, where leading scholars serve as a sort of telescope, outlining, as it were, the anatomy of the field in question. The interviews are designed to capture both the tenets of the field as well as the individual scholar's way into it. In this way, several different layers of the field and its institutional roles are grasped simultaneously: Who are the main figures in the field? What were their motivations for entering the field and what paths did they follow? What do they consider the most important findings of the field, and what do they themselves see as their own main contributions? What is the role of the field in academia, and its connections to neighboring disciplines? And finally, what do they consider to be the most pressing research questions and unresolved issues in the field?

By using the *Five Questions* tool to address such a wide selection of issues, we do not suffer from the illusion of achieving a systematic or statistically valid image, let alone a global coverage of the field as a whole. Rather, what we obtain is a kaleidoscopic view of different, yet connected, observations and arguments concerning the field of images – whose importance is granted by the selection of central figures agreeing to participate.

The questions posed to all participants were the following:

1. Why were you initially drawn to the study of images?
2. What do you consider your contribution to the field?

3. What is the proper role of the study of images in relation to other academic disciplines?
4. What do you consider the most important topics and/or contributions in the study of images?
5. What are the most important open problems in this field and what are the prospects/avenues for progress?

We hope that the set of thought-provoking answers provided in this book will contribute to the further development and integration of the study of images.

February, 2016
Aud Sissel Hoel,
Peer Bundgaard &
Frederik Stjernfelt

Acknowledgements

We are particularly grateful to the contributors for devoting time to writing such erudite, enlightening, and often thought-provoking interviews, and grateful to the philosophical community in general for showing interest in this project. In addition, we would like to thank editor-in-chief Vincent F. Hendricks and associate editor Henrik A. Boensvang of Automatic Press ♦ $\frac{V}{I}$ P.

February, 2016
Aud Sissel Hoel,
Peer Bundgaard &
Frederik Stjernfelt

1

Mieke Bal

Cultural Analyst, Filmmaker, and Professor Emerita in Literary Theory at the University of Amsterdam

1. Why were you initially drawn to the study of images?

There is often an anecdotal answer to such questions. I was doing work on ancient stories (from the Hebrew Bible) and stumbled upon a problem of philology that biblical scholars had not been able to solve — a seeming contradiction. I literally *saw* the solution in a work by Rembrandt on the story I was struggling with. This was the story of Judges 19, the gruesome gang rape and murder of a young woman. Rembrandt made a sketchy drawing of the scene in the story where the husband opens the door and finds his wife unconscious, perhaps dead. The entire rationale of the violence had remained ill-understood, partly because — as I later speculated — the anthropological background of it was unacceptable to an anachronistic bias in favor of modern marriage and partly because the relation between the man and the woman was systematically sentimentalized. Rembrandt's drawing made that reading problematic and thus opened for me the way to a new interpretation, which was well received in Biblical scholarship and clearly solved a long-standing problem. Since then, I keep saying that painters are often the better biblical scholars — simply because they see what they read. A few experiences of that level of anecdote, and my soul was sold to the devil of the image.[1]

I found the image particularly challenging for several reasons. As a literary scholar, I saw how much images "had to say" — what I called at first "propositional content" but later came to consider "visual thought." However, after writing a book on Rembrandt (Bal 1991) in that spirit, I felt compelled to go back to literature and explore how texts are also visual (Bal 1996). So, for me, the visual-verbal opposition is not an opposition at all but a complementary relationship between two textual forms with different possibilities and tendencies.

---

[1] My interpretation of the story was published in a book, *Death and Dissymmetry: The Politics of Coherence in the Book of Judges* (1988), remarkably receiving the 1991 Biblical Archaeology Society Award for the best book related to the Old Testament. I wrote on the Rembrandt drawing in "The Rape of Narrative and the Narrative of Rape: Speech Acts and Body Language in Judges" (1988/1990).

A third step in the development of my interest in images emerged when I began to make films to complement the documentation in libraries about contemporary culture. That which I wanted to understand — how cultures are in permanent change — seemed under-documented, so I began to make films to supplement this meagerness. I have never learned more about people, cultural situations, and the small barely visible things that make up the "look" of, for example, a city. Editing these images, I have learned to look with a near-obsessive, myopic gaze.

2. What do you consider your contribution to the field?

I have been told that the pair of books mentioned above — Rembrandt and Proust — has brought *word-and-image studies* a step further. Because I did not focus on texts with illustrations or images with some words in them, but analyzed the discursive dimension in "purely" visual images and vice versa, the visual imagination at work in the literary art itself, this field moved beyond the somewhat repetitive level of technical analysis to something more profound and generally useful: a semiotics of intermediality. This then also became useful for museum studies, to which I contributed *Double Exposures*. In these books, I also conceptualize the methodological issues pertaining to the analysis of visual images. This development of analytical tools is very important to me because it is democratic. Rather than exposing brilliant interpretations to students — who may enjoy them but feel that they cannot do that themselves — a clear exposition of concepts with examples of how to use them instead *empowers* students. It gives them a feeling that this is doable; that they can do it, too (e.g. Bal 2002).

I think my contributions also include the concept of *preposterous history*, as a historical methodology that is sanguine about our own position in interpreting images (Bal 1999). The anachronistic approach to images is really useful in understanding why it is that we keep so fascinated by old images, and how we connect to these. This became clearer than ever before when Michelle Williams Gamaker and I were invited by the Guggenheim Bilbao Museum to make a video essay. It was to be a commentary on the exhibition of seventeenth-century paintings from the Städel in Frankfurt in that ostentatiously contemporary building. We made a three-channel video installation in which we juxtaposed, opposed, and otherwise confronted with each other details from the old paintings and contemporary video images to explain the potentially illuminating impact of anachronism. The making of that installation helped me to understand better the differentiated kinds of relationships between present and past.

A third area where I have, I think, contributed new ideas is the analysis of the *political* potential of art that is not thematically "about" politics. This is important because the interest in political art has been rather destructive due to a rhetoric of do-gooders who confuse art and propaganda. Adorno already understood so well that political art is a paradoxical endeavor. If it is explicit in its political plea, it is anti-political in that it becomes propaganda, hence, authoritarian. If, however, art is only focused on itself, it is implicitly politicizing but for the cause of a mystifying a-political thought. In each of my books on this question I probe the work of an artist — Doris Salcedo, Eija-Liisa Ahtila, Ann Veronica Janssens — who I think are keenly political, without anywhere in their work making political statements, representing political issues, and the like (Bal 2010, 2013a, 2013b).

These have become dialogic books, where the art was enabled to "speak back," to contribute to the thinking about it. This is also a contribution I have made. Others have spoken of this under the heading of "theoretical objects" (Damisch). But I have contributed novel forms of art writing, taking the consequences of this dialogic attitude in the textual genre adopted. In a "one-artist dictionary," I have written short essays about twenty-six images, named after a concept they inspired (Bal 2008). In the book on Salcedo, five different aspects — metaphor, time, anthropomorphism, space, and installation — are given political shape, so to speak, in the artist's work. In the book on video installation, each of five installations begins a dialogue with the critic-theorist about what it means to make, or watch, a moving image. In the third book of this trilogy, abstraction, usually considered a-political, becomes the starting point of experiences that have political implications.

A fourth area of contribution is the theory-practice interaction. In my recent film projects, I try to publish about the projects in order to explore how practice-based theory and theory-based practice can develop without being in each other's way — art becomes too theoretical, for example, or writing about one's own work becomes defensive or self-indulgent (Bal 2013c).

3. What is the proper role of the study of images in relation to other academic disciplines?

I think this role is increasingly recognized to be tremendously important as well as in need of critical reflection. It requires a visual version of what Appadurai has termed the "research imagination" to assess what visual images contribute to our understanding and, hence, how their study can help other academic disciplines.[2] Others know much

---

[2] Arjun Appadurai has developed this idea in three stages. See Appadurai 1997, 1999, 2000.

more than I do about, for example, medical imaging.³ Clearly, in the empirical sciences, imaging is an important form of analysis. Medical imaging is not only a tool for diagnosis but also an "explanation" from a particular perspective. The images contribute to the ongoing process through which we imagine the human body in particular ways. Just think of the image of a fetus and it is immediately clear how such images can be used to manipulate.

We have witnessed the well-known discussion about the possibility to use images in *history-writing*, for example, sharpened by the question of images of horror and the readability of visible horror. This question has philosophical aspects, about modesty and voyeurism, but also a semiotic one — what is reading, and how can we do it? For me, the skill of reading images is so important because without it, such discussions flounder in the quicksand of Puritanism and group-privilege on one side and on the other: exhibitionism and a sense of ownership.

In *cultural anthropology*, visual images have a long history, first as drawing and painting, then as photography. There, the difficulty is the appropriating quality of photography, the tendency of privileging the colonizing gaze, which leads to exoticizing imagery. The critical analysis of that tradition has sometimes led to disingenuous indignation and the concomitant disavowal of complicity. But with a keen critical sense, and especially with the greater possibilities of audio-visual media, a more dialogic and performative approach to image-making in intercultural contact can also enrich our understanding, not only of that alleged "other," but of the contact itself: how intimacy can be facilitated and the camera used for empowering rather than the opposite. My own video work is centrally devoted to that question.⁴

It may seem a truism to claim that *art history*, too, can benefit from visual analysis — the skill of detailed "reading" of visual images. Still, I think the traditional approaches in that discipline — valuable in their own right — have not always been conducive to a deep understanding of how images work, produce meaning, circulate, and affect people. Moreover, the developments in moving-image making have inflected the notion of image itself, away from iconographic stability towards an audio-visual mixture. *Film and media* studies could not exist without such transformed conceptions of the image. These are just a few examples of academic disciplines where images have far-reaching implications.

---

[3] Cartwright 1995; van Dijck 2005.

[4] See on this question in anthropology the essays in *The SAGE Handbook of Cultural Analysis* (2008). On my video work in this area, see the exhibition catalogue *La última Frontera/The Last Frontier. Obras de Mieke Bal en colaboración con Michelle Williams Gamaker y otros* (2011).

4. What do you consider the most important topics and/or contributions in the study of images?

It follows from the above that I am most invested in an analysis, not of images alone, but of their social functioning. This has several aspects. First, the "impurity" of images — the way they perform beyond the visual alone, in synaesthesia; beyond the individual, and beyond a single cultural community. What matters is what happens in those boundary-crossings; this seems to me a primary issue that we have intuitively sensed but not yet explored in great detail and depth. This also concerns the images written in texts — not just literary ones, but also journalistic evocations and other forms of writing. Few writers integrate the in-depth analysis of images in this cultural-analytical perspective and reflection on this intermediality of (primarily) visual images. My model for this is Kaja Silverman's *Threshold of the visible World*. Mitchell's introductory chapter to *Iconology* remains a key text. Marianne Hirsch analysis of an Holocaust photograph of a child, and Ernst van Alphen's analysis of the visual poetry of Charlotte Delbo, the former in our volume *Acts of Memory*, the latter in his book *Art in Mind*, are inspiring.[5]

Then, I am interested in the impact of images on the political — not so much politics as the institutional domain where consensus is the goal, the means, and the weapon, but the political as the domain where social life happens, where people are allowed and enabled to disagree, to argue, even to fight, so that the presence and agency of images actually matters.[6] Also, the ethical aspect of looking at images comes up, for example, in the case of images of suffering, of pain, but also in the voyeurism that adheres to looking into private lives without the informed consent of the object of the gaze. I consider those ethical aspects meaningful, precisely because they are rather fluid and should not become subject to the rigidity of morality — let alone moralism. I appreciate much of the work of Mark Reinhardt, for example his fine analysis of Kara Walker's work, and the exhibition he mounted in Williams College, MA, with an award-winning book as a catalogue.[7]

The pedagogy of "visual literacy" is a domain I find important, without seeing much in school and other educational programs that feeds the interest of people in visual communication. Leaving the media to themselves is a waste. I think it would be useful to develop curricula in ordinary schools for understanding the potential of what is called

---

[5] Silverman 1996; Mitchell 1986; Hirsch 1999; van Alphen 2005.

[6] For this distinction between politics and the political, I rely on Chantal Mouffe (2005). Under different (and in my view, problematic) terms, Jacques Rancière (1999) makes a similar distinction.

[7] Reinhardt 2003; Reinhardt, Edwards, & Duganne 2007.

the social media, for example, Facebook; and for developing skills in making more interesting pages. This can surreptitiously, so to speak, encourage a deeper understanding of how images "work."

5. What are the most important open problems in this field and what are the prospects/avenues for progress?

The domain of the pedagogy of visual literacy has not, I think, really been studied yet. The term "visual literacy" refers to the skill of "reading" images. The underlying supposition holds that images are no more transparent than texts, and that learning to read them enhances the ability to resist manipulation by means of images, as well as to assess historical and contemporary meanings and aesthetics. It is difficult because it requires collaborative work, between scholars and teachers, as well as between theoretical and empirical analysis. The obvious place for this would be media studies departments.

I also think that the theory-practice collaboration needs developing. The current trend of art-based PhDs can be productive, and I have seen some terrific projects develop. But so far, I fear that, as a trend, let alone a requirement, it is too much administration-driven (the Bologna agreements) and aimed at streamlining: it is not anchored in a profound reflection on the theoretical in art and the imaging in theory. Yet, I have learned more from video making in the past six or so years than from anything I had read in libraries.

These two examples already suggest that my primary concern is all forms of "inter-ship," as I call it: interdisciplinary work, and other collaborative efforts, too frequently hampered by organizational considerations. Moving forwards requires a shift in thinking about individual achievements. This is not accomplished by enforcing team projects, as is the case with many funding agency's policies. For me, interdisciplinary work begins by a serious reflection on what that preposition inter- means. But that may be for another "Five Questions" volume.

Bibliography

van Alphen, Ernst. 2005. *Art in Mind: How Contemporary Images Shape Thought*. Chicago: University of Chicago Press.

Appadurai, Arjun. 1997. "The Research Ethic and the Spirit of Internationalism." *Items* 51, 4, pt. 1: 55–60.

Appadurai, Arjun. 1999. "Globalization and the Research Imagination." *International Social Science Journal* 160: 229–238.

Appadurai, Arjun. 2000. "Grassroot Globalization and the Research Imagination." *Public Culture* 12, 1: 1–19.

Bennet, Tony & John Frow, eds. 2008. *The SAGE Handbook of Cultural Analysis*. London: SAGE Publications.

Cartwright, Lisa. 1995. *Screening the Body: Tracing Medicine's Visual Culture*. Minneapolis: Minnesota University Press.

van Dijck, José. *The Transparent Body: A Cultural Analysis of Medical Imaging*. Seattle: The University of Washington Press.

Hernández-Navarro, Miguel Á., ed. 2011. *La última Frontera/The Last Frontier. Obras de Mieke Bal en colaboración con Michelle Williams Gamaker y otros*. Murcia: Fundación José García Jiménez.

Hirsch, Marianne. 1999. "Projected Memory: Holocaust Photographs in Personal and Public Fantasy." In Mieke Bal, Jonathan Crewe, & Leo Spitzer, eds., *Acts of Memory: Cultural Recall in the Present*, vii–xvii. Hanover: University Press of New England.

Mitchell, W.J.T. 1986. *Iconology: Image, Text, Ideology*. Chicago: University of Chicago Press.

Mouffe, Chantal. 2005. *On the Political*. New York & London: Routledge.

Rancière, Jacques. 1999. *Disagreement: Politics and Philosophy*. Julie Rose, trans. Minneapolis: University of Minnesota Press.

Reinhardt, Mark. 2003. "The Art of Racial Profiling." In Ian Berry, Darby English, Vivian Patterson, & Mark Reinhardt, eds., *Kara Walker, Narratives of a Negress*. Cambridge: MIT Press.

Reinhardt, Mark, Holly Edwards, & Erina Duganne, eds. 2007. *Beautiful Suffering: Photography and the Traffic in Pain*. Chicago: University of Chicago Press.

Silverman, Kaja. 1996. *The Threshold of the Visible World*. New York: Routledge.

Selected publications by Mieke Bal

1988. *Death and Dissymmetry: The Politics of Coherence in the Book of Judges*. Chicago: University of Chicago Press.

1988/1990. "The Rape of Narrative and the Narrative of Rape: Speech Acts and Body Language in Judges." In Elaine Scarry, ed., *Selected Papers from the English Institute*, 1–32. Baltimore: Johns Hopkins University Press.

1991/1994. *Reading "Rembrandt": Beyond the Word-Image Opposition*. Cambridge & New York: Cambridge University Press. Reprint 2006 in Amsterdam: Amsterdam University Press.

1996. Double Exposures: The Subject of Cultural Analysis. London &

New York: Routledge.
1997. *The Mottled Screen: Reading Proust Visually*. Anna-Louise Milne, trans. Stanford: Stanford University Press. In French: 1997. *Images littéraires, ou comment lire visuellement Proust*. Montréal: XYZ Editeur. Toulouse: Presses Universitaires de Toulouse.
1999/2001. *Quoting Caravaggio: Contemporary Art, Preposterous History*. Chicago: University of Chicago Press.
2001. *Louise Bourgeois' Spider: The Architecture of Art-writing*. Chicago: University of Chicago Press. In Spanish: 2006. *Una casa para el sueño de la razón: Ensayo sobre Bourgeois*. Rafael Sánchez Cacheiro & Ángel Paniagua, trans. Murcia: Cendeac.
2002. *Travelling Concepts in the Humanities: A Rough Guide*. Toronto: University of Toronto Press. In Spanish: 2009. *Conceptos viajeros en las humanidades: Una guía de viaje*. Yaiza Hernández Velázquez, trans. Murcia: Cendeac.
2008. *Balthus: Works and Interview*. Barcelona: Ediciones Polígrafa. In French: 2008. *Balthus: Oeuvres, Écrits, Entretiens*. Jean-François Allain, trans. Barcelona: Ediciones Polígrafa. In Spanish: *Balthus: Obras y entrevista*. Marta Pérez Sánchez, trans. Barcelona: Ediciones Polígrafa.
With John Sparagana. 2008. *Sleeping Beauty*. Chicago: University of Chicago Press.
With Miguel Á. Hernández-Navarro. 2008. *2MOVE: Video, Art, Migration*. Murcia: Cendeac.
2009. *Fragments of Matter: Jeannette Christensen*. Bergen: Bergen National Academy of the Arts.
2010. *Of What One Cannot Speak: Doris Salcedo's Political Art*. Chicago: University of Chicago Press.
2013a. *Endless Andness: The Politics of Abstraction According to Ann Veronica Janssens*. London: Bloomsbury
2013b. *Thinking in Film: The Politics of Video Installation According to Eija-Liisa Ahtila*. London: Bloomsbury
With Michelle Williams Gamaker. 2013c. "Scenography of Death: Figuration, Focalization, and Finding Out," *Performance Research* 18, 3 June: 179–186.

2

Gernot Böhme

Professor Emeritus of Philosophy at Darmstadt Technical University

---

1. Why were you initially drawn to the study of images?

In teaching philosophical aesthetics, I gave a seminar on images. This led me to three main topics:

- The origin of image theory in Greek antiquity.
- The difference between *image* and *tableau* and the possible independence of images from media.
- The pragmatics of image.

The outcome of my seminar was published under the title *Theorie des Bildes* (Böhme 1999).

2. What do you consider your contribution to the field?

The origin of the theory of images is not, as usually thought, Plato's story of the cavern but rather his analysis of what a sophist is, in his dialogue *Sophist*. Sophism is the art of deception, i.e. giving images instead of real being. Explaining how this is possible, Plato first gives a definition of what an image is: the other of the true being made looking like it (*Sophist* 240a). Plato's theory of images in his dialogue *Republic* only introduces the difference between true being and representation. This relation is repeated on three levels: between the One itself and the ideas; between the ideas and concrete things; and between concrete things and pictures or shadows. This hierarchy is only a hierarchy of ontological ranking. Contrary to this, the theory of images in *Sophist* takes into account the purpose of imaging and thus refers to practices and methods applied in the art of sculpture and architecture of the time: images are not only made to reproduce something, but also to render an expression to the observer. This is the first example of aesthetics of perception or of rhetoric of imaging.

The difference between image and tableau gives rise to the question whether an image can exist on its own, i.e. independent of material media. This is only possible as digital data — yet, as such, they are not images. Images are only independent of media in that one image can appear in different media. This gives rise to the question of what different media do to an image (Böhme 2004a). This sort of question did not arise before the impressive development of reproduction techniques. Strangely enough, the existence of an image as a data file brings new attention to the material medium on which the file may be printed out (Böhme 2004b). Then there is the question regarding the relation of the image to its frame or to the background upon which it is projected. From this question, there is a link between image theory and scenography — or the art of stage setting (Böhme 2011).

Very often we talk of virtual reality when only images are at stake. Images are only to be called virtual reality if the spectator, in his bodily presence, is in some way integrated into the picture. This is the case with simulators for aircraft training, with perception caves, and with different pieces of art (Böhme 2004c).

One question of great importance is: in which ways do images affect us in our bodily existence? The main example for affection through images is found in the realm of sexuality. In general terms, one can say that images may have the power to organize our bodily constitution. The effect must have its origin in the biological history of mankind (Böhme 2004c).

This point leads to the theory of image pragmatics. The hermeneutics of images so far have only taken into account the horizon, i.e. the context in which an image is perceived. Image pragmatics considers in addition the context of the praxis relevant for understanding a picture. Thus, the meaning of a picture is different depending on whether you take it as a means of identification — for example in a passport — or as a representative of a person beloved. One and the same picture can be understood in a different way depending of the context you make use of it (Böhme 1996a, 1999, 2004c).

In my photographic studies, I made photographs of dawn, dusk, and mist (Böhme 1996b, 2007). My proper contribution to the art of photography is "atmospheric photography." This is not only requested when reproducing a mood or atmosphere, but also in particular to overcome the classical architectural photography which only represented buildings as if they very eternal monuments. Atmospheric photography here tries to give an expression how a building is experienced in the context of life, weather, and seasons.

3. What is the proper role of the study of images in relation to other academic disciplines?

History of arts: here, the study of images may come to balance the prevailing understanding of pictures as complex information — the atmosphere an image radiates to a spectator is decisive.

Cognitive science: the role of images in memory, the organization of the body, and the rising of emotions must be studied.

Scenography and marketing studies: the functional production of images here lies in their contribution to an atmosphere, a climate, and a commodity style (Böhme 2011).

4. What do you consider the most important topics and/or contributions in the study of images?

The ontology of images: their particular status as entities.

The anthropology of images: the study of images as integral parts of everyday life and of their function in community formation — in particular their role in politics.

5. What are the most important open problems in this field and what are the prospects/avenues for progress?

What is mostly neglected is the role of images in the formation of the body, both concerning the physiological status and the actual feeling of a person.

Image pragmatics is a new field; studies here are still rare, although the impression of life as living in and with pictures is overwhelming (2001).

Selected publications by Gernot Böhme

1996a. "Dies Bildnis ist bezaubernd schön…" *der blaue reiter* 3: 69–73.

1996b. "Das Bild der Dämmerung." In Norbert Bolz & Ulrich Rüffer, eds., *Das große stille Bild*, 234–245. München: Fink.

1999. *Theorie des Bildes*. München: Fink.

2001. "Ist die Realität wirklich? Die Bilderwelt gehört zum menschlichen Lebenszusammenhang." *Neue Zürcher Zeitung* May 1999, 19–20.

2003. "Die Wörter und die Bilder bei Magritte." In Dieter Mersch, ed., *Die Medien der Künste: Beiträge zur Theorie des Darstellens*, 117–125. München: Fink.

2004a. "Archäologie der Natur in den Materialbildern von Fritz Vahle." In Susann Kretschmer & Stefan Graupner, eds.,

Medien Experiment Spiel: Festschrift für Fridhelm Klein, 252–269. Wolnzach: Kastner.

2004b. "Das Bild und sein Medium." In Gerhard Johann Lischka & Peter Weibel, eds., *Die Medien der Kunst: Die Kunst der Medien*, 40–65. Wabern: Benteli Verlag.

2004c. "Die Wirklichkeit der Bilder." In Christian Filk, Michael Lommel, & Mike Sandbothe, eds., *Media Synaesthetics*, 84–94. Köln: Herbert von Halem Verlag.

2006a. "Körper, Bilder und Gewalt." In Kathrin Schmidt, ed., Katalog zur Ausstellung *Annegret Soltau – ich selbst*, 152–157. Darmstadt: Mathildenhöhe.

2006b. "Nach-Bilder: Zum historischen ort von Neo Rauchs Gemälden." In Kunstmuseum Wolfsburg, ed., *Neo Rauch — Neue Rollen: Bilder 1993–2006*, 47–50. Köln: DuMont.

2006c. "Die Wirklichkeit der Bilder und ihr Gebrauch." *JTLA Journal of the Faculty of Letters* 31: 1–12.

2007. "Dunstbilder." In Gerhard Gamm & Eva Schürmann, eds., *Das unendliche Kunstwerk: Von der Bestimmtheit des Unbestimmten in der ästhetischen Erfahrung*, 235–248. Hamburg: EVA.

2011. "Die Kunst des Bühnenbildes als Paradigma einer Ästhetik der Atmosphären." In Ralf Bohn & Heiner Wilharm, eds., *Inszenierung und Vertrauen: Grenzgänge der Szenographie*, 109–117. Bielefeld: transcript.

3
Marta Braun

Director of Photographic Preservation and Collections Management at Ryerson University

---

1. Why were you initially drawn to the study of images?
I was the eldest child in a bookish household — my mother was a journalist — so I grew up looking at images in books, from board books and illustrations in classic story books to lavishly illustrated museum guides full of paintings and sculpture (where I encountered my first pictures of naked bodies) and of course, comic books. TV only came into my life relatively late — my parents resisted it longer than most — while movies were a weekly habit. I think that I'm a living example of Marx Wartofsky's theory that we learn to know the world only after we have seen images of it.

In a more formal way, I was drawn to the *study* of images because of my being allowed to study a particular group of images — photographic negatives by Etienne-Jules Marey discovered under the roof of the Institut Marey in Paris. These were scientific images for which I had no context for understanding. They were difficult to decipher; it was hard to comprehend what was being represented in them. I was drawn to these images because I wanted to grasp their meaning. After ten years of studying them, I found these images even more interesting than when I first saw them. And they led to my study of another very specific group of images, those in Edweard Muybridge's *Animal Locomotion*.

2. What do you consider your contribution to the field?
If anything, I have contributed to an expanded history of photography. But to explain, I need to trace the history of photography from the 1980s when I started to study these negatives. Back then, the market for photography was taking off: important museums were staging large monographic exhibitions as they expanded their collections and university courses in the history of photography were being established as part of humanities curricula. All this attention, however, was on photographs that could be considered 'art' as defined by the formalist tenets of modernism. Thanks to critics who insisted on an expanded field for

the study of photographic images, the history of photography today includes just about any kind of photograph as a suitable object of inquiry, not just the photograph as a work of art. Within that history, I believe that my contribution has been to provide a context for Marey's images, to situate them in a history of scientific inscription rather than a history of artistic production and to show that Muybridge's work was not scientific, as usually thought. And because my studies of Marey and Muybridge have brought to light their treatment of race, gender, and class, I hope that I have contributed something to the broadening of those streams in the field.

3. What is the proper role of the study of images in relation to other academic disciplines?

I'm not sure I understand this question. Since images are important, if not key, to illustration and explanation in both the sciences and the humanities, I would think that their proper role would be at the center of most academic disciplines. But images also have agency — they can create or change positions and arguments. So visual literacy includes more than the ability to decipher images, it also supposes an understanding of agency, of how images circulate, how they mutate, and how they get consumed. I essentially agree with W. J. T. Mitchell's rigorous relativism: that the image has its own agency with different meanings in different disciplines, but that it is culturally specific. The proliferation of digital images and the almost infinite possibility of their transformation or mutation in this increasingly globalized society requires that the specificity of those cultures becomes more clearly understood.

4. What do you consider the most important topics and/or contributions in the study of images?

Plato's contribution — his ideas about the pleasure images provide and their capacity for deception still seems to provide a compelling topic of image study in the work of Guy Debord et al. The study of visual rhetoric, including semiotics, has merged more recently with affect theories and researchers who have sought to connect the study of images to the study of brain function and memory. The digital revolution has made the topic of replication/transformation and circulation of images more important than ever.

5. What are the most important open problems in this field and what are the prospects/avenues for progress?

To continue from the previous question: although much has already been accomplished in this area, we still don't know why or how images seduce us either from a sensory or a semiotic view. Further research has to be done in the neurology of vision, including unconscious vision and the manner in which images validate the naturalness of vision. How neuroscience will contribute to the study of images is certainly an open problem. The effects of the commodification and consumption of digital images is something that is only partially studied. As for prospects for progress, I'm confident that the solutions to such problems are being found as I write.

Selected publications by Marta Braun

1992. *Picturing Time: The Work of Etienne-Jules Marey 1830–1904.* Chicago: University of Chicago Press.

2005. "Chronophotography: Leaving Traces." In Nancy Matthews, ed., *Moving Pictures: The Un-Easy Relationship between American Art and Early Film, 1890–1910*, 90–95. Williamstown MA: Williams College Museum of Art.

2007. "Aux limites du savoir: 1845–1900; la photographie et les sciences de l'observation." In André Gunthert & Michel Poivert, eds., *L'Art de la Photographie des origins à nos jours*, 139–79. Paris: Citadelles & Mazenod.

2010. *Eadweard Muybridge*. London: Reaktion Press.

2014. "Giacomo Balla, Anton Giulio Bragaglia, and Etienne-Jules Marey." In Vivien Greene, ed., *Italian Futurism, 1909–1944: Reconstructing the Universe*, 95–103. New York: Solomon R. Guggenheim Museum.

4

Horst Bredekamp

Professor of Art History at Humboldt University, Berlin

---

1. Why were you initially drawn to the study of images?
After the war, my parents were thirsty for all the elements of culture that had been forbidden under the Nazis. They bought all the books on modern art they could afford, and they became members of one the "film clubs" in which avant-garde films were shown. One Sunday morning in the 1950s, they took me to a matinee of Henri-Georges Clouzot's film about Picasso, showing the artist drawing and painting the most astonishing metamorphoses behind a glass screen. That was the initial moment for me, at the age of seven.

2. What do you consider your contribution to the field?
In the last forty-five years, the tradition of Aby Warburg's art history as a general history of pictures — "Bildwissenschaft" in its purest sense — has regained its status as one of the important wings of art history and I have tried my best to contribute to this process. In the tradition of art history that goes back to Franz Kugler, Gottfried Semper, Jakob Burckhardt, Alois Riegl, and many others, I have tried to cover all historical periods and media from late antiquity to the most recent movements of our time. My fields of specialty were and are the history of sculptures, the history of modern visual media, the art of collecting, political iconography, and the interrelation between science and the arts. Ultimately, the connection between art history and philosophy has become a major issue for me (from Leibniz to modern concepts of embodiment).

3. What is the proper role of the study of images in relation to other academic disciplines?
Whoever deals with images properly in their materialized forms of *pictures* learns that each shape is individual and concrete, and that one has to accept the dignity of the smallest detail before one proceeds to theories. Each particular is first taken as an exception and not as an example of norms, terms, and signs: herein lies the difference between art history

and aesthetics, as well as some parts of literary history, which in the last decades has been in danger of losing its subject. The adequate study of images is a schooling in being both concrete and theoretical.

The image-based disciplines of archeology and art history have created methodological tools of systematic description, comparison, collection, interpretation, theory of style, and iconology, which have always been models for other disciplines, such as biology (Darwin and Haeckel), psychoanalysis (Freud), film history (Arnheim), and the history of literature (Curtius & Jauss).

The other side of the coin shows that, without other disciplines, images can never be fully understood. This is why the history of science, the history of religion, philosophy, and language theory, to name but a few fields, play a fundamental role in art history as shaped by Warburg, Edgar Wind, Erwin Panofsky, Ernst Gombrich, and many others.

4. What do you consider the most important topics and/or contributions in the study of images?

One of the most demanding topics is the reconstruction of a world art history as it was once established by Franz Kugler's most liberal "Handbuch der Kunstgeschichte" (1842). The problem will be to avoid creating a "mishmash" of the visual cultures of all times and instead to shape the abundant material using philosophical tools.

To give an example: up until now, it has been an open question whether the archeological and art-historical tools of "Bildwissenschaft" are universal or purely products of Western culture. It is my experience that these methods are affirmed and accepted without any pressure by any other culture that begins to shape its own history through "Bildgeschichte." It seems as if the methods of stylistic analysis, comparison, and iconology could be more readily compared to the history of physics than to hermeneutics. One example for this might be perspective, which, notwithstanding concepts that counter central perspectivity, shaped one possible universal approach to the reflection and construction of space. But this is an open debate that might be answered only after generations to come.

5. What are the most important open problems in this field and what are the prospects/avenues for progress?

The increasing sensibility for images in fields other than the traditional disciplines has led to one of the most important developments in contemporary academia, enriching the study of images immensely. It is of greatest importance that images are accepted not only as illustrations but also as constructions of what they represent.

On the other hand, however, they are often still treated as "Bildchen" that can be manipulated at will. As the practical problems of presentation show in a paradigmatic way, the skill needed for this analysis and use of imaged have not yet been acquired. Often images are shown in lecture halls that cannot be darkened, projected onto frames that create parallaxes and on which shadows are cast by the auditorium, they are confronted with simultaneous representations of texts that are added to or even overlap the pictures, next to other kinds of mutilations. Pictures are often treated as if one were analyzing a poem after having cut off the last words of each line.

The greatest problem in image studies is the lack of skill and material-based knowledge. The most dramatic effect can be observed in the sciences that, to a certain degree, have become picture disciplines, without however knowing how to treat, store, collect, archive, and analyze pictures. Without a method that cares for the value of even the most modest image, each progress made in the study of images will be only superficial.

If these problems are solved, a culture might be created in which, for the first time since the Byzantine period of iconoclasm, images will be accepted and reflected as what they are: fundamental tools of shaping and reflecting the technical, scientific, and playful aspects of the world.

5

James Robert Brown

Professor of Philosophy at the University of Toronto

---

1. Why were you initially drawn to the study of images?

I heard about Galileo's thought experiment involving falling bodies when I was a beginning undergraduate. It was the most wonderful thing I had ever heard. As a beginning philosophy student, I had read Plato and Descartes and loved them both. Hume I found deflating, but was resigned to thinking empiricism must be right and rationalism a mere delusion. Then came Galileo who turned all this upside down. There seemed hope for old-fashioned rationalism after all. I thought about visual reasoning from time to time since then, but never got into the topic until I had a regular academic job. It was in the mid-1980s that I plunged in. I planned to read as much as I could on the issue and set out to collect material. What shocked me then (and still does) is how little had been written on the topic. Of course, there were lots of thought experiments, but almost nothing in the way of theorizing about them. Mach, Koyré, Kuhn, and a handful of others exhausted the literature. At the time, about 25 years ago, one could master it all in a long weekend. Since then, the situation has changed enormously.

As well as thought experiments in philosophy and the sciences, I had a longstanding but independent interest in mathematics. Once one becomes convinced of the power of thought experiments in the natural sciences and philosophy it follows on rather naturally to start thinking of things that are similar to thought experiments and visual reasoning in mathematics. After finishing my book on thought experiments, *The Laboratory of the Mind*, I started to work seriously on visual reasoning in mathematics and began collecting examples of visual proofs. Others had similar thoughts in mind. Roger Nelsen produced two books called *Proofs Without Words* (I & II). Anyone interested in picture proofs in mathematics will find them invaluable.

2. What do you consider your contribution to the field?

Not much beyond pointing out a few nice examples. Since I'm likely the only Platonist writing on these matters, I'm probably useful as a foil for others. John Norton might say something similar. He and I occupy the pole positions on a spectrum — he's at the extreme empiricist end while I'm the rationalist outlier. Many writers on thought experiments will discuss and dismiss our two views, then go on to locate themselves somewhere in between, which, of course, looks very reasonable. Norton, like me, is happy to perform this public service, though we agree that all "moderate" views are wrong. I'm reminded of a remark once made by Bernard Shaw that the typical middle class Englishman is moderately honest, moderately faithful to his wife, and so on.

If I were to be a bit more specific in what I think I've done — without saying these are actually noteworthy contributions — I would include some of the following: (1) Lots of examples of thought experiments, described in enough detail that they are useful for others to begin their own work. (2) A taxonomy of thought experiments. Since they work in many different ways, rival accounts of thought experiments are usually right about some cases, but I doubt that there could be any simple account that captured them all. Even my own Platonistic account only deals with a few rather unusual cases. (3) Tying thought experiments to a realist account of laws of nature and to the epistemology of intuitions in the philosophy of mathematics. (4) Collecting examples of picture proofs in mathematics and trying to make the case for their legitimacy as genuine evidence, not just heuristic devices. There may be a few others, but this is a reasonable sample.

3. What is the proper role of the study of images in relation to other academic disciplines?

I think this is an open question. Physicists have long taken thought experiments seriously, but neither they nor anyone else has much in the way of a theory about how they work or why we should trust them. Philosophy counts on thought experiments extensively, too. There has always been some worry within philosophy about such examples. After all, they might just be an expression of our deeper prejudices, especially in ethics examples. The last 25 years have seen a significant growth of interest in the nature of thought experiments. The number of articles, conferences, and PhD theses devoted to the topic continues to grow. So we should see some significant progress in all sub-fields in the next few years.

Particular fields might focus on different aspects. There is, for instance, an interesting question about the relation between thought experiments and works of literary fiction. Both have a narrative structure in which we see what happens and both draw morals from this. Whether the connection between novels and thought experiments is deep or superficial is yet to be determined; though some fine work has been done by David Davies, Catherine Elgin, and others. If we take a very different example, chemistry, the situation is quite perplexing. Unlike physics, which is loaded with thought experiments, chemistry seems to have few or even none at all. Why is this? What is it about chemistry that discourages a kind of reasoning that is so prevalent elsewhere? If we could answer this question, I think we would learn a lot about the discipline of chemistry and the difference between it and physics.

4. What do you consider the most important topics and/or contributions in the study of images?

This is a nearly impossible question to answer — at least for me. There have been major advances in the neurosciences, in aesthetics, in the depiction of designs, and so on, as well as advances in the relatively narrow area in which I work. It would be hopeless for me to weigh them against one another. Within the area of thought experiments, I would list a few the achievements of my fellow philosophers and historians of science. John Norton, whom I mentioned earlier, has proposed an account of thought experiments that would satisfy any staunch empiricist. He claims that a thought experiment is an argument (or can be reconstructed as one). It is a good argument in so far as it is deductively or inductively valid. If it passes the logical test and also has empirically justifiable premises, then it is a good thought experiment. I think his account works very well for a number of cases, but I don't believe it for a moment when it comes to others. There are additional approaches. Nancy Nersessian and Nenad Miščević have independently proposed an account based on mental models. They both go a long way in explaining a number of important examples, but I'm not persuaded of the account in general. There are several others who have or who are in the process of advancing our understanding of thought experiments greatly. James McAllister, for instance, has argued that various factors need to be in place and sometimes have been in place in order for thought experiments to be possible.

When it comes to mathematics, there is growing interest in the role of diagrams and the possibility of picture proofs. Jon Barwise and Marcus Giaquinto, for instance, have both written a lot on the topic, though neither is as persuaded as I am that some picture proofs really are proofs.

5. What are the most important open problems in this field and what are the prospects/avenues for progress?

The number of open questions is enormous and I'm quite optimistic about future research.

1. The number one problem about thought experiments is the old one: How is it possible that just by thinking we can learn something new about the world? In some respects, this question recapitulates the

long-standing debate between empiricists and rationalists. Current debates about philosophical methodology are intimately related, even if they do not mention the term "thought experiment."

2. What are the different ways in which thought experiments can work? My own efforts concerning taxonomies is at best just scratching the surface; much more work, based on many more new examples, is needed.

3. The history of thought experiments needs cultivating. I can imagine lots of great books with titles such as: Galileo's Thought Experiments, Thought Experiments in the Work of Einstein, The Role of Thought Experiments in the Development of Quantum Mechanics, Thought Experiments in the Middle Ages, A History of Ethics through Thought Experiments, and so on. I'm not going to write any of these, but I hope others will. In each I happily promise to buy a copy.

4. Are literary fictions (novels, plays, movies) a kind of thought experiment? A handful of people have started to address this problem.

5. Disciplinary differences: Why do some fields, e.g., chemistry, have few or no thought experiments, while others, e.g., physics and philosophy, have so many? Any answer to this question will inevitably tell us a great deal about the disciplines involved; there are bound to be deep differences waiting to be revealed.

6. Can diagrams in mathematics, which are invariably of special cases, provide genuine proofs of theorems? And if they can, how do they manage to do this? This is where intuition seems to come into play. What is it about some diagrams that trigger powerful intuitions that advance mathematics significantly?

7. Some mathematical notation is remarkably powerful on its own. Knot theory, for instance, has several notations that are useful for treating different situations, some of these combine pictures right in the symbolism itself that are somewhat reminiscent of hieroglyphics. Remarkably, this is topic is quite unstudied. What is the relation to more standard uses of language? What is the semantics and syntax of diagrams?

This is just a sample of some of the questions that I think are interesting and important. I am delighted that a growing number of other people are finding them exciting, too.

Selected publications by James Robert Brown

1986. "Thought Experiments since the Scientific Revolution." *International Studies in the Philosophy of Science* 1: 1–15.

1987. "Einstein's Brand of Verificationism." *International Studies in the Philosophy of Science* 2: 33–54.

1991a/2010. *Laboratory of the Mind: Thought Experiments in the Natural Sciences*. London: Routledge Second Edition.

1991b. "Thought Experiments: A Platonic Account." In: Tamara Horowitz & Gerald Massey, eds., *Thought Experiments in Science and Philosophy*, 119–128. Lanham: Rowman & Littlefield.

1999/2008. *Philosophy of Mathematics: A Contemporary Introduction to the World of Proofs and Pictures*. London & New York: Routledge.

2003. "Why Empiricism Won't Work." *Proceedings of the Philosophy of Science Association* 2: 271–279.

2004a. "Why Thought Experiments Do Transcend Empiricism." In Christopher Hitchcock, ed., *Contemporary Debates in the Philosophy of Science*, 23–43. Malden: Blackwell.

2004b. "Peeking into Plato's Heaven." *Philosophy of Science* 71: 1126–1138.

2005. "Naturalism, Pictures, and Platonic Intuitions." In Paolo Mancosu, Klaus Frovin Jørgensen, & Stig Andur Pedersen, eds., *Visualizations, Explanations and Reasoning Styles in Mathematics*, 57–73. Dordrecht: Springer.

2007a. "Counter Thought Experiments." *Royal Institute of Philosophy Supplement* 61, 82: 155–177.

2007b. "Thought experiments in science, philosophy, and mathematics." *Croatian Journal of Philosophy* VII: 3–27.

2007c. "Comments and Replies." *Croatian Journal of Philosophy* VII: 249–268.

2013. With Yiftach Fehige. 2013. "Thought Experiments." *Stanford Encyclopedia of Philosophy*. http://plato.stanford.edu/entries/thought-experiment/

Forthcoming. "Das »Gedankenexperiment«: Die Diskussion der letzten 25 Jahre." *Deutsche Zeitschrift für Philosophie* 59.

6

Matthias Bruhn

Art Historian, Research Associate, and Head of the research group "Das Technische Bild" at Humboldt University, Berlin

---

1. Why were you initially drawn to the study of images?
When I studied Art History in Hamburg, Germany, there was no such thing as *Bildwissenschaft*. At least no one seemed to have heard of this word, even if similar or related terms, like *Bildkunde*, already existed in History and Ethnography, and even if various sub-disciplines and fields of research and education were dealing with images practically and theoretically (like pedagogy, esthetics and others). As a matter of fact, people could have heard of a so-called *image science* established by physicists in the mid-1980s due to the demands of astronomical and large-scale laboratory research that required persistent means for the storage of huge amounts of electronic information, comparable to what is know known as 'big data.' Yet the German term *Bildwissenschaft* was only slowly emerging in the late 1990s, and the teachers I had encountered adopted it only reluctantly, since their focus was entirely different.

As a result of the 1970s revolt against right-wing representatives of art history (some of them even active during and after the Nazi era without interruption) and due to a particular interest in the exiled scholars of the Weimar republic, my curriculum included authors like Warburg and Panofsky, Hauser and Benjamin. It covered political themes and the social backgrounds of art, and fields like *Visual Communication* were interpreted in terms of ideology critique and the mechanisms of mass-media imagery. Guest lecturers and assistant professors taught French poststructuralist philosophy, gender issues, and video art. In many ways, it was already a much broader perspective than what is now considered to be *Bildwissenschaft*.

For the same reason, and in contrast to the emphasis of epistemological reformation, the scholars I met remained somehow dismissive of any attempts to turn art history into a variant or subdomain of *Visual Culture Studies*. Due to this bias, I realized only with a certain delay what issues they addressed, what canon of (European) high art they supposed to overcome, or what kind of research in the history and hegemony of vision and "visuality" they were to pioneer instead. It took me some time to learn that it was not for reasons of ignorance and conservatism but for reasons of disciplinary history that German colleagues never considered it a limitation to call themselves "art historians," even if they conceded that others often understood "art" in a much narrower sense. It had never come to their mind that Renaissance festivities, the Panorama and Diorama, photo archives or computer screens would or should *not* be part of art history. My own dissertation was thus a book on the correspondence of French classicist painter Nicholas Poussin, focusing on recurring patterns and seemingly banal details in his letters, including e.g. comments on his poor health, or lack of money.

Regarding the alleged objectives of visual culture studies, language proved to be another barrier of communication. A *Bild* can be a piece of carved wood, a photographic print on paper, or a digital file. The original German/Germanic term comprised the diverse concepts of *eidolon* and *eikon,* representation and likeness — thus 'images' (mental, electronic) as well as 'pictures' (manually made, materially present) would be included. As a long-term result of industrialization, however, *Bilder* are now commonly identified with paintings, photographs, film, or electronic media, i.e., assumingly flat, rectangular, screen-based phenomena. *Bildwissenschaft* is therefore more likely to be taken as a translation of *Visual Culture Studies* — or misunderstood as in methodological opposition to studies in "material culture," suggesting that the first is devoted to the study of visual "forms" (patterns, motives) and the latter to the materiality of "things."

On the other hand, with the rise of illustrated books and press photography around 1900, *Bild* has finally become the multi-functional term for representation and evidence in many fields — which is why Aby Warburg or Walter Benjamin have thought and spoken of themselves as "picture historians" (*Bildhistoriker*) in order to express that the ambivalent modernization of society manifests itself in a visual memory that should be conceived as a permanent communication of mental, even unconscious or neglected images rather than as a collection of a few selected works of high art. Many languages have adapted to this process, as can be deduced from the irritation that people feel when photographic depictions of war and disaster are described in terms of art and design. For the same reason, the label *Bildwissenschaft* has become attractive to art historians who may be aware of such historical discourses but also wish to indicate that they take contemporary phenomena and new kinds of images into consideration.

2. What do you consider your contribution to the field?
During and after my dissertation, I partly worked in the local branch of a U. S. American stock photo agency where services and pictures

(slides!) were organized and provided according to professional demands like speed, price, and availability. I started to realize that the processes within and around such photo libraries — then still the leading institutions for the mass distribution of pictures — represent principles of a global picture market as well as its profound transformation caused by digital photography and the rise of the *world wide web*. Digital multiplication had begun to challenge the traditional notion of pictures, copyright protection, and intellectual property. New market leaders appeared, offices were closed and slide collections replaced by CDs, soon followed by Internet servers.

Taking over the direction of Martin Warnke's "picture index," located in Aby Warburg's former library in Hamburg, gave me an opportunity to see some effects of this transformation also in the scholarly field. The "index" contains a huge collection of more than 300,000 reproductions, brought together in order to establish a catalog of political motives in visual communication and to analyze to what extent political demands and actions have fostered the evolution of modern artistic strategies. In contrast to traditional (mythological, religious) iconographies, the collection did not start from given key words and taxonomies. Instead, it developed keywords and taxonomies by sorting a growing amount of small-scale reproductions according to gestures, attributes, assumed functions and other aspects.

About this time in the late 1990s, it became clear that black-and-white photographs were a receding means of art historical research. New media would be essential not only for the digitization and dissemination of a given art historical knowledge, but also for its very definition. Would it change the community's visual memory when paintings or architectures were represented digitally (perhaps even in 3D) instead of the usual photographs? How would scholars respond to video footage, DVDs, pattern recognition software, or hypertext structures as tools of research? At the same time, logistical or legal limitations quickly became obvious, not to mention the everyday trouble with showing video files in a classroom.

In such a context, the term *Bild* also conveyed another meaning, namely as the common denominator for problems occurring within this permanent visual exchange. It is obviously the umbrella term for an extreme variety of genres and media. Scanning a book page, producing a porn movie, or setting up a digital archive are entirely different tasks — but they are subsumed under the generalizing notion of a "picture" whenever they are to be treated and commodified as a professional material. So despite the terminological possibility to distinguish drawings from prints, photograms from pictograms, and TV from video, and despite the separate professions and technologies behind them, "picture" has become the unit of measure to count and compare very different expectations and claims towards visuality, thereby defining a material through particular ways of its production, distribution, and consumption. If it were not about the "pictureness" of the picture but about patterns or media, more precise terms would be available for that purpose. "Picture" may be a mere simplification and abbreviation used by everyone for reasons of verbal economy. Interestingly, it happens to describe a particular quality of an object, i.e. the layer of licenses and intellectual properties.

Like in earlier ages, when iconoclastic movements had fostered the dispute about the legitimacy and value of "the image" in society, and like in the early modern era when the privilege or authorship of a certain design was connected with a particular *idea* or *concetto,* the *Bild* behind *Bildwissenschaft* can now stand for a shared interest in a uniform object or commodity. As Tom Mitchell has rightly stated, there are no "visual media," at least in theory, as long as visuality is always a multi-media phenomenon; still there will be "visual media" as long as there are people earning money with the demands related to the term. I decided to call this process a *Bildwirtschaft* ('economy of pictures'), a word composite that, unfortunately, is hard to translate into English since it can both be comprehend as the picture trade as such as well as a 'pictorial economy,' suggesting that picture and economy explain each other mutually.

The exploitation of pictures, be it a resource of creativity, a printing permission, or an asset type, is neither a decline nor a progress, but an integral part of the evolution of a concept and the permanent re-constellation of pictures, words, and other symbolic forms in the history of media. Like spoken language, images (or pictures, patterns, symbols, decorations) have been means of trade and communication since mankind began to use tools. Pattern and logic may not be the same; but there is no definite, absolute border or distinction between pictures and non-pictures. Depending on cognitive factors, but also on contexts, grammars, or practices (writing, drawing, crafting), some signs are preferably regarded as letters or words, and others as depictions or motives. The letter "I" can stand for "one," for a "line," or for a complex ideogram, and a signature is both a drawing and a sequence of letters. Economies of exchange, on the level of goods and on the level of their representation, foster the progressive distinction of symbolic systems concerning readability, reliability, or artistic quality, and due to the mechanisms of this exchange, e.g., to the materials employed and the icons controlled by authorities, pictures, and money, visuality and economy remain closely linked. Pictures of every kind, ranging from coins, statues, and illuminated manuscripts to charts, photo snapshots, TV, and Internet streams have become a reality in their own right, fueled by social expectations and technological innovation.

3. What is the proper role of the study of images in relation to other academic disciplines?

As a consequence, pictureness remains hard to define, and should thus be deconstructed historically – just like it is possible to speak of "art" on the condition that it describes a particular historical situation with particular objects, professions, forms, and places of production and perception. *Bildwissenschaft* will hardly be confined to the ontological question of what class of phenomena should be related to the words image or picture, regarding the metamorphosis of terminologies and the changing objects they comprise, for in the process of industrialization, the meanings of descriptions like *icon, picture, illustration,* and *film* have changed considerably. The evolution of new media has permanently restructured the genres, formats, and means of (re)production; it has brought up new artistic professions and styles, and created and fostered new iconographies.

On the other hand, while there may be no such thing as a definite image or picture, there is nevertheless an industry of first-, second- and third-order producers, of art critics and theorists, legal experts, and technicians accompanying this activity. Even art history is a result of it. Since the discipline was once established to identify objects or qualities worth being preserved in a world becoming fragile or massificated (leading to well-known criteria like artistic "quality" or historical "importance"), it was already forced, a long time ago, to discuss the relativity of terms like art, beauty, value, taste, or to explain why a few luxurious works made for princes and patricians should represent the entire society or epoch in which they emerged.

This discussion is an important part of its knowledge. For we may find ourselves puzzled again by the immense visual productivity, analog and digital, and by the *richesse* of literature devoted to them. In such a situation, *Bildwissenschaft* seems to offer a solution, at least to German speakers. But there may not be a unified discipline soon, even if textbooks suggest there was, because in clear contrast to its solid title and even if more and more institutions include the buzz-word into their own curricula, it will not only remain an endless and faceted domain like the domains of *visual culture studies* but also the territory for contradictory claims, generalizing political statements, and a great deal of academic vanity to explain the entire world in a new key. Would "image studies" be about theory at all, or would they rather circumscribe an "applied" science? Then again, would they also teach how to make better porn movies? Or to optimize political advertising? If not, why not?

For practical and conceptual reasons there won't be a holy alliance to answer problems in a joint effort. Neither the humanities nor the sciences can give up their methodologies only in order to become part of a larger field of study. They will rather prefer to contribute to it as major players. In return, disciplines like art history or archaeology that have once been established in response to comparable historical situations seem prepared to declare *Bildwissenschaft* their paramount occupation and perhaps go so far as to change their denomination. At least they will able to act as important auxiliary disciplines for the sciences and the humanities in that they offer approved methods to access the vast fields and complex processes of visual production.

4. What do you consider the most important topics and/or contributions in the study of images?

What is an image? It's a five-letter-word, used in English and French. Conceding this terminological restriction, images could be found simply everywhere. Formulae, charts, tables, diagrams, maps demonstrate how far graphic informations of different quality interact and intersect, and in consequence there's no scientific discipline that wouldn't use them in research and education. Yet astonishingly enough, many scholars still neglect or mistrust images in theory, while using them in practice every day. There are several reasons for this reserve.

As mentioned, images / pictures are now commonly identified with certain media and formats, which are again prone to all kinds of abuse, e.g. in religious propaganda or totalitarian political systems, to fraud, or to exploitation and commercialization. They are thus identified with a certain class of objects, although their functions, techniques, and media have clearly diversified and specialized. As a result, they are reduced to a primitive, lo-fi, homespun expression that only affects emotion but misses logic. A fundamental misconception behind this attitude is that images are polysemic and open to interpretation, while words are exact code. They aren't. Letters can be indecipherable, words chance their meaning, they deceive and discriminate, and the division of national languages has made it impossible for many people to communicate with each other directly. Have words ever been abandoned just because they are used for lying?

Just like in language (and despite its codification in academies and dictionaries), meaning in images is created through individual interpretation and use. And just like in Ferdinand de Saussure's concept of language, meaning in images is defined by difference — be it the difference between motives, between media, or between beholders. The black-and-white photograph will show reality in a different way than the color one, and knowledge is what lies between them. It's the surplus of their co-existence.

In the assumed case that images are equivalent to other systems of differentiated expression, like verbal language, then their understanding should not be based on a few simple rules either. On the contrary, they are a challenge comparable to learning foreign languages — a competence that does not become superfluous by the theoretical knowledge what language "is." A theory of images will not exempt the scholar from analyzing the diversity of the visual, its media, purposes, participants; it takes a trained memory, a sense for detail, a knowledge of techniques and materials, an awareness for the individuality of perception, for the power of market processes or political institutions.

The *iconic turn* was to express a respective change in attitude, assuming that pictures have decisive epistemological values and aesthetic qualities. However, when representatives of this recent research trend deal with the systematic question of what their object of study consists of, they often seem to avoid discussing the old-school socio-economic approach of ideology critique that had been the fundament for studies in mass imagery in 1970s art and cultural history, ethnography, photo history, and many other fields on international level. Of course, economic or social histories are only one perspective, too, and economically speaking, the original artwork reproduced in the book can either receive increased attention through multiplication or lose attention through repetition. Yet without wanting it, theorists neglecting this research tradition by pretending that Bildwissenschaft is *the new thing* may even foster the idea of pictures as a commodity by reducing them to an alleged theoretical core.

In this respect, *Bildwissenschaft* is not a question that will ever get an answer, but perhaps the title for a new training or education similar to the "school of seeing" that inspired enlightened pedagogues, modern reformers, *art scientists*, and design theorists around 1900, each of them trying to respond to new sensations, quantities of production, dialects of visual expression. Even if a uniform *Bildwissenschaft* was able to comprise all the issues mentioned, including psychological, theological, and mathematical questions and aspects, it would hardly deliver straightened formula exemplified by a few chosen objects that some scholars agree upon as sufficient for their theory-building. Such a discipline would run the risk to become even more normative than the allegedly old-fashioned art history it pretends to modernize. History is messy, and words and pictures are historical.

5. What are the most important open problems in this field and what are the prospects/avenues for progress?

Yet in view of the long chronicle of versatile experiences and practices, "picture theory" stands for a high degree of abstraction concerning the level of discussion, which may be due to common expectations that (a) images can be defined in absolute terms and (b) there is a true world behind them. But there isn't. Graphic structures are part of the same world they are meant to depict. Often enough, they are not meant to depict anything. As science sociologist Knorr-Cetina has shown, speaking of "discourses" will no longer be sufficient when it comes to a basis in fact that is itself visual. Visual information is generated during the process of communication and across the boundaries of media and contexts; diagrams conceptualize thoughts and ideas; models do model a virtual reality. It is a fundamental insight of art historical research that pictures of any kind must be considered as tools in their own right, no longer to be underrated as additive decorations or as simplistic visual explanations for those who can't read. Like the spoken word, visualizations should not only be estimated in epistemic terms of evidence or truth alone, but also in the rhetorical terms of virtue or impact.

In consequence, the notion of "form," colloquially understood as the surface of a substance, being the opposite of a given "content," a weak translation from the logical to the sensuous, has to be reloaded. The shape of a mathematical curve or the color of a medical image is nothing arbitrary; it is as meaningful as the staged appearance of a politician in public, or the quantity of a TV broadcast that reaches billions of households, or the "artifact" appearing on a CT screen. This meaning is connected to history and society; it is neither purely theoretical nor cognitive.

The bigger the number of pictures, the more apparent it becomes that they do not equal the entries of a dictionary but the words spoken. Which is why the iconographic order of a picture book is not a hidden grammar behind them — there is none — but only one way among others to rank and sort the material, just like a dictionary explains a word by giving a couple of new ones. A picture can represent figures and gestures, but it can also appear as a black square; as a black square, it can both represent basic Gestalt principles as well as avant-garde art theories. A picture drawn on paper may become a means of knowledge, of personal memory, of cultural heritage, or of intellectual property, not despite but because of the fact that it is related to the contexts that charge it. If this is true for the meaning of a word within a sentence, it should also be valid for the meaning of a pattern within a painting.

Any psychological analysis of visual perception is forced to reduce the parameters and factors of an experimental test-situation by using simplified graphic structures that appear on a flat screen; in the end, such precise test situations do not reveal the mechanisms of "pictures" — even if they employ some — but the mechanisms of their cognitive processing. Likewise, if image studies were to understand and discuss a theory of images, they should at least discuss how a topic or a concept like "the image" could become as current and important as it is nowadays. Etymological and comparative research would be as essential as studies in the history of key institutions (such as academies, galleries, publishers, archives), dominant media, formats and techniques, collections and classifications, iconographies and styles. This is a task partly unfinished, but to a large part already performed — by a project once called "art history."

Selected publications by Matthias Bruhn

2003. *Bildwirtschaft. Verwaltung und Verwertung der Sichtbarkeit.* Weimar: VDG.

2003. "Visualization Services. Stock Photography and the Picture Industry." *Genre, Forms of Discourse and Culture* 36, 3/4: 365–381.

2008. *Das Bild. Theorie – Geschichte – Praxis.* Berlin: Akademie.

With Vera Dünkel. 2008. The Image as Cultural Technology. In James Elkins, ed., *Visual Literacy*, 165–178. New York: Routledge.

2010. "The Iconology of Power. A European Perspective on Political Imagery." In Benjamin Drechsel & Claus Leggewie, eds., *United in Visual Diversity: Images and Counter-Images of Europe*, 17–33. Innsbruck: Studienverlag.

2011. "Life lines: An art history of biological research around 1800." *Studies in History and Philosophy of Science* part C, 42, 4: 368–380.

2012. "Pictures of a Higher Order." In Nina Samuel, ed., *The Islands of Benoît Mandelbrot. Fractals, Chaos, and the Materiality of Thinking*, 83–89. New York & New Haven: Yale University Press.

Co-Editor of *Bildwelten des Wissens. Kunsthistorisches Jahrbuch für Bildkritik.*

7

James Elkins

E.C. Chadbourne Chair of Art History, Theory, and Criticism at the School of the Art Institute of Chicago

---

1. Why were you initially drawn to the study of images?

Growing up in a household that was intensively dedicated to natural history, I was surrounded by dozens of natural history guides and monographs, binoculars, telescopes, collections of shells, bottles of algae, spiders, insects of all sorts, mushrooms, leaf samples, bee hives, snakes, mice to feed the snakes, scorpions, caterpillars, petri dishes, nets for plankton, nets for butterflies, nets for fish, sampling containers, dissection equipment, display cabinets, potsherds.

Later, in college, I trained as a painter; I have an MFA in painting. The painting was appalling — made outside of any engagement with the contemporary — but the experience of coming from art practice into art theory, instead of from art theory toward practice, was formative.

2. What do you consider your contribution to the field?

I wish I could say. I think I have worked to broaden the subject matter of art history and visual studies, but both fields continue to look mainly at fine art and popular culture images. My work hasn't had the impact that, say, Tom Mitchell's has for three reasons: because I have continued to work with a late-romantic interest in the limits of representation; because I continue to be unconvinced by attempts to make a distinction between art and non-art (I have no special allegiance to, or interest in, art); and because for me, the act of seeing continues to be essentially a private experience, so I find myself uninterested in the many kinds of social viewing and identity construction that comprise the principal part of current research. I think my impact has been diffuse and local, and therefore not centrally important.

3. What is the proper role of the study of images in relation to other academic disciplines?

Images continue to be used as illustrations of arguments. Their "proper role," if that's the right expression, would be a fuller one in which images would also propel and guide arguments, suggest their own arguments, interrupt or slow arguments, contradict arguments, and otherwise do work of their own aside from exemplifying arguments. There is a fair amount of rhetoric — especially in visual studies but also in science — that says images play this sort of formative role, but I do not think it happens very often. In the humanities, for example, writers like Susan Buck-Morss have said that images guide their arguments, but I remain unconvinced. The overwhelming majority of writing in visual studies, art theory, aesthetics, art history, Bildwissenschaft, and related fields employs images as illustrations, mnemonics, instances, or exemplars of positions taken up in the accompanying texts. To see this, consider how unusual it would be to read a sentence like this: "My argument about the gaze, which I have been drawing from Jean-Paul Sartre, Jacques Lacan, and Maurice Merleau-Ponty, is undermined by this image, which casts some of these theoretical positions into doubt." For me, the "proper role" — by which I mean the most interesting, powerful role — of images would be one that is very different from current practice. It would be a role in which images themselves help redirect and articulate the concerns of art history and related fields, instead of exemplifying those concerns, or being illuminated by those concerns.

4. What do you consider the most important topics and/or contributions in the study of images?

Perhaps the most important topic, because it is the most capacious, is the relation between images and thought. In different accounts, images have been said to contain non-linguistic meaning, to contain linguistic meaning, to possess "iconic logic," to be non-propositional, to be fully propositional, to be "in discourse," to be apart from discourse, to be "pensive," to be like language, to elicit thought, to contain thought, and to argue. The list of writers who have wrestled with this issue is almost the same as the full list of modern and contemporary theorists: Nelson Goodman and Charles Peirce of course, but also Louis Marin, Hubert Damisch, Jean-Louis Schefer, Jacques Rancière, Erwin Panofsky... the list is endless because the topic is so poorly conceptualized. Theories range from semiotics to animism, from visual communications to visual essentialism: the relation of thought and image is the largest looming unresolved issue for the current century.

5. What are the most important open problems in this field and what are the prospects/avenues for progress?

I'll answer the second question, because I've just answered the first. Prospects include:

a. Attempts by scholars as different as John Onians and Catherine Malabou to blend vision science with the humanities-based scholarship of vision. The diversity of approaches and bibliographies among the relatively few scholars who read vision science is fascinating: why should Onians's ideas be so different from Wilfried van Damme's, or David Freedberg's? What does it mean when Barbara Stafford and Catherine Malabou hardly have any readings in common?

b. Attempts to speak openly, reflectively, and productively about the relation between images and belief. Here again there's a huge diversity: David Morgan, Marie-José Mondzain, Geng Youzhuang, and Pepe Karmel have almost nothing in common, except their interest in religion and art. Hopefully, as the century progresses, people will become more accustomed to speaking about religion, belief, theory, and history together, and a new discourse will emerge. There are beginnings of this movement visible now: Jennifer Doyle's *Hold It Against Me;* Eve Meltzer's *Systems We Have Loved.*

Bibliography

My best scholarly work is quite different from my best writing. My best scholarship is in *The Domain of Images* and *On Pictures and the Words That Fail Them*. My best writing is idiosyncratic, as all writing should be: *What Painting Is,* and *What Photography Is*. I am currently moving into writing and out of art history, visual studies, theory, and criticism; the reasons are given in detail here: tinyurl.com/k8rxas5.

8
Groupe μ
Liège University

---

1. Why were you initially drawn to the study of images?

Back in the 1960s, stimulated as we were by Jakobson's famous article about metaphor and metonymy, we took rhetoric as our first subject of study. However, we immediately gave a general status to this discipline (hence the title of our first work: *A General Rhetoric*, 1970). This led, as a matter of course, to a work program in which we examined successively specific aspects involved by the use of rhetoric in various human activities.

The poetic field was obviously a priority choice, in view of the current situation in linguistic studies, the existence of an available sophisticated specific vocabulary, and also the renewal in rhetoric studies that materialized in Perelman's works, which did not satisfy us at all. This field was covered quite quickly with our *Rhétorique de la poésie* (*The Rhetorics of Poetry*, 1977). On the other hand, four of the six members of the initial group were in close connection with the world of plastic arts and visual techniques, and an interest in plastic and iconic languages was present from the start.

That is why the image was chosen as a second field — but it turned out to be more complex, notably owing to the absence of a specific vocabulary and especially of clearly established concepts. It is no exaggeration to claim that if we exclude Christian Metz and Umberto Eco's generous suggestions, those Nelson Goodman formulated from the philosophical field and some other suggestions by aestheticians, then that which went under the name of visual semiotics was largely limited to some subjective criticism of art, which appeared in the intimidating disguise of an often obscure and, in any case, inaccurate jargon that utterly lacked general theoretical tenets. We might even consider that the situation has not changed in this respect. Therefore, a new theoretical frame had to be elaborated. It took us no less than 15 years to prepare a correctly structured *Traité du signe visuel* (*Treatise of the Visual Sign*, 1992). Indeed, in the meantime, our aim had become more firmly semiotic, and we thought more and more that it required a cognitivist basis. To us, the notion of figure had to be spread in that direction and, for instance, could not go without a theory of pragmatic interactions: we had to overcome Ricoeur's spiritualist psychologism. Simultaneously, we were looking for powerful operations that would demonstrate the general rules of signification and communication and would be likely to engender, in all categories of utterances, phenomena of polyphony comparable to those we observe in verbal language.

In view of the power of the channel they occupy, visual signs present a significant diversity of manifestations: artistic images, of course, but also subway plans, printed circuit boards, montage plans, scientific images, and diagrams of all sorts, including the moving images of cinema and television. In the face of such diversity, added to that of linguistic utterances, of music, and other systems of signs, a new common denominator imposed itself: that of signification and its origin. It is at that time that cognition, which had first merely been an adventitious question, turned out to be crucial. Indeed, if it was at a pinch possible to build a rhetoric of the poetic function (to use its Jakobsonian name) without worrying about the psychophysiology of audition or of phonation (which, retrospectively, really seems less defendable to us today!), it became really impossible with the image, which continuously sent us back to rods, cones, pigments, and to the neuronal architecture which they feed. Our *Treatise* shows this necessity, still addressed shyly at this stage: we will see in our answer to question five that it is the whole semiosis that our current research reconsiders from this angle, from an accurate and general definition of sense, in order to clarify mental operations of which the essential enigma is to put together the following triple aspect: (1) to arise from senses; (2) to be non-modal; and (3) to preserve however the trace of their sensory origin.

2. What do you consider your contribution to the field?

After meticulously listing the visual sign dimensions (shape, hue, saturation, brightness, texture), we tried to find a formal structure for each as well as characteristics likely to bond them directly to signifieds. For instance, do natural signifieds of color really exist? Such automatic connections turned out to be rare and limited. On the contrary, the biggest freedom seemed to reign in the creation of signs as well as in the reference to real or imaginary signifieds.

A crucial achievement of the *Treatise of the Visual Sign* (which Göran Sonesson said was to visual communication what Saussure's *Course in General Linguistics* was to linguistics) was to distinguish plastic signs from iconic signs and to establish two classes of autonomous signs, both containing a content plane and an expression plane, therefore allowing to think the first in their specificity, and not only as serving the second. The "plastic level" (which in the Peircian taxonomy can sometimes play the role of a symbol and sometimes that of an index) has three parameters: form, texture, and chromaticity, with each of these parameters having its own modalities of articulation, syntactical relations, and semanticisation. As to the "iconic level," it is the one we traditionally describe by a similarity between the signifier and the signified, or motivation (we will hereafter consider how this should be qualified).

A very productive singularity of the plastic/iconic distinction was the study of their interaction, which we have called icono-plastic, and which has been presented by Herman Parret as a major contribution. Therefore, what distinguishes art from the simple mimetic copy of the world — as well as how other types of images function: advertising images, scientific images, mobile images, etc. — was clarified in a simple, productive, and original way.

Henceforth, it became possible to design our planned visual rhetoric by distinguishing a plastic rhetoric, an iconic rhetoric, and an iconoplastic rhetoric. And this might be considered a third contribution to the field of research. Until then, rhetorical concepts had indeed been transposed to the image without any kind of control. So when you talked about "visual metaphors," the phrase was a mere reproduction of linguistic terminology and its occurrences could refer to drastically different phenomena. From now on, our suggestions make it possible to tabulate permitted rhetorical operations on the visual sign, which, for instance for the iconic sign, are the following:

	Conjuntion	Disjunction
In præsentia	Interpenetrations	Couplings
In absentia	Iconic tropes	Projected trope

Regarding the purely iconic signs, we wanted to formulate a precise description of the so-called "motivation" phenomena. The solution to that tricky matter was made possible by adopting a quadratic (and no longer triadic) structure to describe the sign. This pattern, which had been elaborated by one of us, Jean-Marie Klinkenberg, in his *Précis de sémiotique générale* (*Compendium of General Semiotics*, 1996 and 2000), introduces the *substrate* in the structure, that is to say the material aspect of the signifier. Henceforth, we can share out arbitrary relations and motivated relations without any contradiction between the different components of the sign. Then, the concept of *transformation* makes it possible to provide a technical description of the facts of motivation. The place where motivation is put into operation in the iconic sign is defined: it takes place in the relation between the substrate and the referent. Indeed, these two elements are commensurate (they have dimensions, chromatic and textural characteristics, etc.) and their connection can be established in rigorous terms. It is that establishment of pattern that we called transformation, this concept being our fourth contribution. There are four types of transformations:

- Geometric transformations, operating on spatial properties. That is to say, for instance, proportional transformations (which play with dimensions but preserve angles), projections (which explain all the cases where we have a three-dimensional referent through a bi-dimensional substrate), or topological transformations (which only preserve general characteristics like "open" or "closed," "inside" or "outside").

- Analytical transformations, which apply the processes of algebra to geometry and therefore provide a model representation of spatial phenomena that can have an endless number of values. For instance, discretization permits to go from a continuum to a representation where the entities are clearly separated from one another (think about the equivalence between the Cathedral of Rouen as painted by Monet — with its blurred focus — and the line drawing that can be abstracted from it to illustrate a tourist guide) or even the filtering processes that apply to the three parameters of color and explain the production of monochromes.

- Optical transformations, which operate on the products of reflection and refraction phenomena. It is here that we find contrasts, which can be accentuated or softened, or operations related to the focusing and field depth.

- Kinetic transformations are obtained through a modification of viewpoints. Anamorphosis, for instance, is produced through a lateral displacement of that viewpoint.

But transformation is not enough to define the iconic sign (at a pinch we can transform anything into anything); another condition is required, which consists in maintaining the function of reference, what we have named *co-typie* in French (co-typicalness). Nevertheless, the nature of this *co-typie* is cultural — and this is where arbitrariness may step in.

Ultimately, we see that, far from questioning the possibility of iconicity, as Umberto Eco or Nelson Goodman do, we have come to formulate various degrees of iconicity. Of course, this contribution — the fifth — is not only about the theory of the image, since the issue of motivation has been one of the most recurrent themes in semiotic debates since the origins.

The important question about the connection between sensory experience and signification had already been raised at the beginning of the twentieth century by Charles Sanders Peirce. But, given the knowledge of cognition (and in particular of visual cognition) at the time, he was unable to provide an answer. The originality of the Groupe μ contribution was to create a link between these disciplines and semiotics, a discipline all too often caught up in the dogma of immanentism. It indeed showed that meaning develops from elementary percepts, integrating and organizing stimuli from specialized perceptive mechanisms, in an abstracting approach the purpose of which is to categorize experience.

3. What is the proper role of the study of images in relation to other academic disciplines?
The image intervenes in nearly all human activities resorting to signs: sciences, art, technique... The image is present in those activities both as a document with empirical origin (source image) and as a tool of conceptualization or interpretation (working image). Thus, it is essential to know its nature, its functioning, and its limits.

The reasons for this universal recourse to image are various. The visual channel capacity is seven times bigger than the sound channel capacity. Moreover, the image is permanent whereas sound vanishes quickly: therefore, it constitutes a memory support that extends significantly the thickness of the present (which is approximately 10 sec only, with 16bits/s, so 160 bits). Eventually, by presenting easily topological, figural, or conventional relations, images powerfully complement natural languages and even formalized languages such as logics and mathematics. This can be observed not only at the level of communication but also at the level of heuristics, where the diagram really helps formulating new theories.

At some point or other, most scientific activities contain a processing and an interpretation of images. When it comes to source images (microbiology and astrophysics heavily rely on them), the danger of crediting an artifact with a probative value always exists. The history of sciences shows cruel examples of this. Derivative documents, like recording charts, are prone to mistakes in perspective due to the choice of scales and units. In all those cases, the constraints related to the perceptive system come into play and risk leading the interpretative process in a wrong direction.

Finally, we should not underestimate the often essential part played by illustration in the teaching of sciences and techniques.

4. What do you consider the most important topics and/or contributions in the study of images?
Hereafter, we mention the works that really seem innovative to us. Some consider the image in all its aspects; others restrict themselves to the more limited (but not simpler) field of artistic image. It is easy to understand that we prefer the first ones.

Many renowned researchers dedicated themselves to the study of images, but few did more than scholastically apply pre-existent patterns. This is how we find, ad nauseam, Saussure's binomials, Peirce's triads, and Greimas' semiotic squares. Sometimes, having a key and wanting at any cost to arrange the image in the shape of a keyhole makes the analysis become ridiculous, as when Dora Vallier strives to apply Jakobson's consonantal and vocalic triangles to Malevitch's work. Such an objection cannot be raised against Jean-Marie Floch or Félix Thürlemann's works. On the contrary, they have shown the efficiency of the tools developed by Greimas in their analysis of such complex works as those of Kandinsky or Klee.

Among those who really helped improving our knowledge of images we will mention first — credit where credit's due — Umberto Eco. Although he was trained in aesthetics, he was one of the first to voice the demand for a general theory about the meaning of the image. He never ceased to go back to essential issues such as motivation. But even if we agreed with him on his first critical processes, we could no longer do so when it came to his radical criticism on the concept of motivation, and we consider that its concern about the opposition between ratio facilis and difficilis is something of a headlong rush. He was also one of those who contributed to lead semiotics in a cognitive direction; even if, once more, his answers are still excessively shy.

Göran Sonesson's contribution is both valuable and singular. His encyclopedic knowledge enables him to have a never-failing critical point of view: he immediately detects the weaknesses, the contradictions, and the gaps — not to mention the mistakes — in the proposed theories (ours included!). One of the originalities of his position is the interest he has always shown in philosophy and in the theory of knowledge, along with his concern to avoid speculation by always putting theories to the test of particular images.

Georges Roque, who especially takes up with the artistic and advertising image, also possesses detailed knowledge. This enables him to have an exact count of semiotic concepts without ever forgetting the creators' aesthetic plans. He is doubtlessly the one who, among contemporary specialists, gets closest to the semio-aesthetics whose lack is frustratingly felt. It is in the field of color that his research demonstrated the most significant results.

Hubert Damisch's explicit plan was to establish a semiology of art, trying to express in that specific field the functioning of signifier systems and the mechanism of signification as well as the "work" of reading. This kind of approach provides him with an easy access to nonfigurative art, an access refused to Panofsky.

When it comes to lab works, we must underline David Marr's productive intuitions. It is to him we owe the first convincing clarifications of neuronal mechanisms (or at least of their mathematical equivalents), leading to the saliency of *contour* in perception. Combined with René Thom's theories, those results enabled a full reformulation of *Gestalt* psychology in less conjectural terms. Further from the lab, we will also praise Jean Petitot's works, which take up refining the mathematical contours of those theories.

Finally, Jacques Fontanille's contribution must be vigorously highlighted. It was decisive in the different turn recently taken by French structuralism. This trend, which consequently assigned itself "post-Greimasian," turned its focus to "forms of life" and sensoriality, therefore breaking — although not entirely — with immanentism and autonomism which ruled over Parisian visual semiotics.

5. What are the most important open issues in this field and what are the prospects/avenues for progress?

For us, the most important avenues of progress lie in a better knowledge of vision and of the brain. The acquired knowledge in the vision of colors already enabled a better understanding of the concepts of complementarity, transparency, etc. Optical illusions and camouflage, far from being mere objects of wonder or entertainment, were choice material for this kind of research. The construction of a three-dimensional vision is now also almost clarified, especially thanks to Christopher Tyler's random dot stereogram invention and the systematic uses David Marr made of them. We will notice that the cesia, the recently discovered fourth dimension of the color, is still being explored in practice as much as in theory.

With a less direct import, yet likely to help understand man's relation to the image, the study of vision in more primitive beings — down to cells that respond to the presence of light — must be encouraged.

Significant issues focusing on the nature of the coding of visual information in order to produce mental entities such as concepts also remain. In 2000, Martin Skov wrote, "One of the great puzzles of cognitive science is understanding how [...] phenomenology arises from neurobiology. We know something about the physical process involved [...] (through neurobiology) and something about the formal and semantic aspects [...] (through phenomenology, semiotics and related disciplines), but we have a long way to go in connecting the first to the latter."

Another type of question of a more pragmatic nature that we think must be tackled is that of persuasion through images. While we are widely credited with a contribution to the development of a visual rhetoric, we have to admit that it is above all a figural rhetoric. Even though the figure, far from being a free ornament, plays a significant argumentative role (as we have shown), a lot of work must still be done in order to establish a body of doctrine dealing with this aspect of the visual discourse. However, having such a theoretical instrument seems to be crucial in a civilization of the image like ours. Certainly there are plenty of works dealing with advertising, journalistic or television discourse, the use of images in scientific demonstration or popularization, as well as in deception and cheating, but they are still too empiric in spite of suggestions such as Roque's. The recent conference of the International Association for Visual Semiotics (Venice, 2010) was precisely about the application of the concept of argumentation on images and enabled us to see that there was still a long way to go.

This leads us to a third desirable development: our society needs what could be called a pedagogy of the image. Young Europeans, even those that are barely literate, spend a thousand school hours manipulating concepts related to articulated language. In comparison, how many hours are devoted to the phenomenon of image? Very few. Yet, when we approach this field late in the day, how often is this approach really sectorial (for example when it is limited to history of art) and, above all, referential? Whenever its plastic aspect is considered, it is especially with a technical perspective (color techniques for instance). The explanations for that state of things are multiple: ideology of "transparency," for which the image would give a direct access to the world, age-long disregard for the techniques which seem to involve the body... Obviously, there is an urgent need for us to think about giving citizens weapons that will help them not to be fooled by what constitutes one of the most powerful instruments of their control on the world.

9

Robert Hopkins

Professor of Philosophy at New York University

MY LIFE IN IMAGES

1. A Little History

I first became interested in images while a graduate student at University College London. At the time (the later 1980s), philosophy in Britain was coming to the end of a period in which the philosophy of language was seen as the heart of the discipline. Philosophy studies ideas, yet there is nothing more to ideas than their expression in language. A proper philosophical understanding of language is thus essential to, perhaps even the major part of, answering all other philosophical questions. That, at least, was the wisdom at the time. On the promise of that wisdom, a large-scale research programme was undertaken, inspired by the work of Donald Davidson.

None of this really captured my interest. Joining a research programme has never much appealed and, besides, I struggled to keep in focus my sense of why the Davidsonian approach mattered. I found myself instead drawn to the study of images and in particular at first to pictures, the physical images we use to represent things. Here was a form of representation quite different from language, with its own capacities, delights, and limitations. Moreover, after language, pictures are surely the next most important representations we have. Pictures are everywhere in our culture: on television screens, on advertising billboards, in instruction manuals, and on signboards. Surely they deserved at least a little philosophical attention too?

My interest sparked, I discovered I was in a position to benefit from two pieces of good fortune. The first was that UCL had an expert in the field, Malcolm Budd. I was thus able to have as supervisor someone who was and remains a wonderful guide to the area and a serious contributor to the subject. The second was that the field turned out to be relatively underexplored, compared to many in philosophy, but that what work there was had been done by some major thinkers, including Edmund Husserl, Ernst Gombrich, Nelson Goodman, Richard Wollheim, James Gibson, Kendal Walton, and Christopher Peacocke. With such stimulating material to work with and against, I was hooked, and my fascination with pictures has lasted to this day.

2. Some philosophy: physical images

On the approach I favour, the key to a philosophical understanding of pictures lies in the way we experience them. Pictures are made to be seen and the way we see them is central to how they represent their objects. When we look at a picture, we of course see the picture itself — the marks on the paper, light pattern on the screen, or whatever the materials of which the image is composed. But if this is all we see, we do not understand the picture. Understanding what the picture represents involves being visually aware of something else, in addition to the materials: we must also in some sense see the scene depicted. This is what is distinctive about representation by pictures (and related symbols, such as sculptures). Understanding written language, for instance, does not require us to be visually aware of anything other than the words.

This approach to pictorial representation was developed by Gombrich (1960) and Wollheim (1980, 1987). I am not the only contemporary thinker to advocate it. Three things are distinctive about my work on the topic (1998, 2003, 2004). First, I have tried to think the approach through in more depth than my predecessors. I have, for instance, used the approach to explain certain key features of pictures, such as that they always represent their objects from a point of view, they only misrepresent them within certain limits, and they are destined to represent those objects in at least some detail (a 'picture paints a thousand words'). And I have tried to specify exactly what the relation is between what it is appropriate to see in the picture and what the picture represents.

Unlike my predecessors, I deny that the two always perfectly coincide. Second, I offer a distinctive answer to the central question facing the approach: in what sense do we 'see' what the picture represents? I claim that seeing things in pictures is a kind of experience of resemblance — we see the marks as resembling the depicted object in outline shape. Here is not the place to go into the details of this idea. Suffice to say that it sets me against views such as Gombrich's in which seeing the object in the picture involves, at least in part, an element of illusion (Gombrich 1960, Lopes 2005). In my opinion, we neither believe the object is present nor that anything in our experience tempts us to believe that. Our experience does not, even in part, represent the object as really there. Rather, experience presents the object as there only in the perceptual organisation we find the marks to bear. It is given not as real, but as something like a pattern in what is really before us.

The third thing I have tried to do is to develop the approach so that it not only tells us what is distinctive about pictorial representation in general, but also describes the different sub-species of that genus. We see things in all pictures, and in some closely related representations such as sculptures; but the particular form that experience takes varies from one kind of representation to another. For instance, the way we see photographs differs from the way we see handmade pictures, such as drawings and paintings. This, I claim, is because only in the photographic case is our experience guaranteed to be accurate, and thus we feel related in a particularly intimate way to the facts photographs capture (2012). Again, our experience of some drawing and painting is 'inflected,' so that what we see in the marks can only be captured by reference to the marks themselves (2010a). Our experience of sculpture differs from that of pictures, not merely in that the representations are themselves experienced as being three-dimensional, but also, perhaps, in that they do not present their objects from a point of view (2004, 2010b). And our experience of traditional cinema, made by photographically recording actors on sets, does not always reflect the film's history. Sometimes we see the moving images before us as the photographic record, not of the events filmed, but of the story the film relates (2008). Here, at least, there is an element of illusion in our experience of pictures.

Refining the experiential approach in this way takes us from investigating the nature of pictorial representation to investigating the aesthetics of the various forms that representation can take. For, while not every photograph, drawing, or motion picture is aesthetically interesting, those that are so often achieve this by exploiting the resources their particular media afford. If there is something distinctive about, for instance, representation by photographs as opposed to handmade pictures or by sculptures as opposed to pictures, we would expect at least some artistic achievements in those media to be shaped by them. An artist is someone who taps the distinctive resources of her medium and the differences above capture some of the most fundamental resources the various pictorial media have to offer.

3. A little more philosophy: 'mental images'

This is a good point at which to introduce the other major form of image that has captured my attention, those of the mental variety. There is a long history in philosophy and psychology of assimilating mental imagery to physical pictures. This tendency is also present in everyday thinking: if we visualize some scene, we naturally enough describe the result as a 'mental image' or 'inner picture.' I think these assimilations are serious errors. In fact, I don't even believe there are such things as 'mental images:' it is a mistake to reify the products of our imaginative activities in this way (Sartre 2004). However, while there are no mental images, and thus no inner *things* that could be analogous to physical pictures, there are certainly visual imaginings. These are states in which we visually represent to ourselves the world (at least, ways the world might be). They thus play a role at least loosely analogous to that played by pictures. Just as we can produce physical representations that are linguistic or pictorial in form, so we can represent the world to ourselves in pure thought or in imagistic form. Moreover, while it is odd to compare a mental state with a physical thing, it is far less problematic to compare visualizing with our *experience* of pictures. How does the visual awareness we have of something when visualizing it compare with our awareness when seeing it in a picture? Indeed, how does either of those compare with the visual awareness we have when we see such a thing face-to-face? Those questions are both well-formed and interesting. Thus, despite being fully alert to the dangers of assimilating the two, I extended my inquiry into 'images' to include the nature of visualizing.

The three kinds of visual awareness now on the table — seeing, visualizing, and seeing things in pictures — exhibit both common features and striking differences. The key common feature lies precisely in their visual nature. What makes them visual, and how do they differ from their analogues in other senses — from, say, imaginings that are auditory or tactile (e.g. imagining sounds or feels) and from physical images in auditory or tactie form (e.g. sound recordings or sculptures for the blind)? The question of how to distinguish the senses is one with a long history, reaching back at least to Aristotle. Previous discussion has, however, focussed exclusively on the perceptual case. Once one broadens the question to include the sensory nature of imaginings and physical images, the dialectic shifts interestingly. Some familiar answers no longer look feasible. This is true, for example, of Aristotle's thought that to each sense there corresponds a special sense organ. Other answers look less plausible than before — for example, the popular idea that what distinguishes the various senses is the particular properties each represents: colour for vision, sound for hearing, and so forth. My suggestion is that the hallmark of the various spatial senses lies in the varying perspectival structures in which they represent their objects. Visual awareness involves many points in space being represented in relation to, though separated from, a single point, the 'point of view.' Tactual awareness involves the experience of points in the space explored *being in the same place* as points on the exploring body, so that points touched and points touching are always related one-to-one. And auditory awareness takes a third form, in which the places where sounds are heard to be is experienced either as in the same place as, as spatially separate from, or as between the points from which they are heard (the ears). Unlike the rival accounts mentioned above, these claims can be shown to hold not just for perceiving in a given sensory mode, but also for imagining in that mode (see 1998, ch.7).

If we turn to the differences between the three awarenesses, the most important distinction is between imaginative and pictorial awareness, on one side, and, on the other, perceptual awareness. In my view, in perception objects in the world are experienced as before the mind. Our perceptions may be mere representations, accurate or otherwise; but that is not how they present themselves to us. Rather, they seem to offer us direct contact with the world, so that the nature of experience itself appears constituted, in key part, by the nature of mind-independent things. Perceptual states are thus not experienced as representations, not even representations that are guaranteed to be accurate. They do not acknowledge enough of a gap between their nature and that of the objects perceived for the notion of representation, accurate or otherwise, to be in place. Things are quite different in visualizing and pictorial awareness. Here, the object visualized or seen in the picture is not given as really before me, and certainly not given as a constituent of my experiential state. These awarenesses wear their representational nature on their sleeve. It is explicit in experience itself that we have mere picturing of the world, not unmediated contact with it.

Unresolved issues and other disciplines

I mentioned that there is a temptation to assimilate visualizing to picturing by treating the former as involving 'mental pictures.' An even more powerful tendency, in both philosophy and psychology, is to assimilate visualizing to perceiving. The father figure of this line of thought is Hume, or at least the Hume those in the grip of the tendency find in his writings. He insists that visualizing and seeing are much alike, barring differences in etiology and variations in 'force and vivacity.' Against Hume we can set Ryle, Wittgenstein and Sartre, who argued, persuasively to my mind, for various crucial further differences between the two. I see my work on imagining as an attempt to preserve and develop this anti-Humean tradition. However, the Humean position has a powerful hold in psychology, and there are certainly many interesting empirical results that can be taken to suggest that visualizing is simply the active production of perception-like representations. Settling just how far this evidence supports the Humean view, and clarifying quite what is at stake in these debates, is one important area for future work. As I see things, in pursuing such questions, philosophy and psychology have much to learn from each other. Psychology and the other empirical sciences of the mind throw up valuable data that any account of visualizing (and other forms of sensory imagining) must accommodate. But there is also the question how to relate this data to the life of the mind as we know it from within. Giving an accurate and systematic description of the various forms of experience as we live them is a delicate business that on the whole has been most rigorously pursued by philosophers. Reconciling the third-person account of the phenomena offered by science with the first-person perspective from philosophy should be a collective endeavour, with each party open to the insights the other has to offer.

The methodological situation is much the same when it comes to empirical work on our experience of pictures. Here too there are various questions about the nature of that experience that ought to be amenable to empirical investigation. There is, for instance, the phenomenon known to artists as 'losing the surface.' When this happens, the viewer continues to see the marks that compose the picture as marks, but no longer perceives them as spread across the picture's surface. Instead, they are seen as distributed in three-dimensional space, occupying the form of the depicted object. (If you've never had this experience before a painting, consider watching an animated movie in 3D. What looks to be before you are things distributed in three-dimensional space, only not real things, but drawn versions of them.) This experience of pictures complicates the dialectic between the account of pictorial experience I favour and the position of my Gombrichian opponents. For when the surface is lost, we neither seem to see the object depicted (since we are aware of the marks as marks) nor do we see the marks on the surface as resembling something else in outline shape (since we do not see the marks as distributed on the surface). It would thus be very interesting to know how common such experiences are, and whether they are paradigmatic or peripheral cases of pictorial seeing. While the issue seems too delicate to have been tested empirically as yet, one can only hope that philosophers, psychologists and artists will together find ways to settle the issue.

These issues are not worth investigating simply for their own sake. I doubt we will have a proper understanding of any of the three experiences given pride of place above — seeing, visualising, and seeing things in pictures — without an understanding of the other two. Since the topic of perception is central to both the philosophy and psychology of the mind, resolving some of the outstanding issues in the study of physical and mental imagery is a means to wider ends, as well as an end in itself. I have already suggested that the study of physical imagery is also important to the aesthetics of the various visual arts. I hope this sketch of some of the central questions that have occupied me since I began serious research in philosophy will provoke others too into thinking about them.

Bibliography

Gombrich, Ernst. 1960. *Art and Illusion: A Study in the Psychology of Pictorial Representation*. London: Bollingen.

Goodman, Nelson. 1968. *Languages of Art*. Oxford: Oxford University Press.

Selected publications by Robert Hopkins

1998. *Picture, Image and Experience*. Cambridge: Cambridge University Press.

2003. "What Makes Representational Painting Truly Visual?" *Proceedings of the Aristotelian Society Supplementary* LXXVII: 149–167.

2004a. "Pictures, Phenomenology and Cognitive Science" *The Monist* 86, 4: 654–676.

2004b. "Painting, Sculpture, Sight and Touch." *British Journal of Aesthetics* 44, 2: 149–166.

2008. "What do we see in film?" *Journal of Aesthetics and Art Criticism* 66, 2: 149–59.

2010a. "Inflected Pictorial Experience: Its Treatment and Significance." In Catharine Abell & Katerina Bantinaki, eds., *Philosophical Perspectives on Depiction*, 151–180. Oxford: Oxford University Press.

2010b. "Sculpture and Perspective." *British Journal of Aesthetics* 50, 3: 1–17.

2012. "Factive Pictorial Experience: What is really special about photographs?" *Nous* 46, 4: 709–731.

10

John Hyman

Professor of Aesthetics at the University of Oxford

---

1. Why were you initially drawn to the study of images?
I read Ernst Gombrich's wonderful book *Art and Illusion* in 1981. I'd completed my BA a few months earlier, and I was spending a year in Geneva on a scholarship, before returning to Oxford to begin the BPhil. The topic in philosophy that interested me most at that time was perception, and I was struck by the extent to which Gombrich's arguments relied on views about visual perception that he had inherited from the Helmholtzian tradition in psychology, and therefore indirectly from Locke and Kant. I thought that arguments in the philosophy of perception exposed serious mistakes and confusions in this tradition and that they could therefore shed important light on the fascinating questions about pictorial art that Gombrich discussed in his book.

2. What do you consider your contribution to the field?
One of the main results of pursuing this line of enquiry was that I discovered that twentieth century ideas about Renaissance perspective and about the techniques for depicting space and light that were invented in the ancient world depended crucially on a theory of visual perception, which stemmed from the advances made in optics in the seventeenth century and still dominates the scientific study of perception today. The theory is that visual perception is the result of interpreting retinal images — the screen images objects in the visual field produce in our eyes. Helmholtz thought this process of interpretation was similar to reasoning or making inferences, in which the logical steps are governed by laws of association, drawn from the experience, which begins in infancy, of moving our limbs and bodies with our eyes open, and touching or bumping into things. Psychologists now think of it as making computations, in which the logical steps are governed by algorithms that are partly innate and partly the result of learning. But the basic idea is the same.

The influence of this theory on art history was immense, because it led psychologists and art historians to believe that shading, foreshortening and perspective are successful techniques for depicting solidity and depth because pictures that use these techniques resemble retinal images — the pictures our visual system has evolved to interpret. Now this cannot be right, because a painting which really did resemble a retinal image would be painted upside down on the inside of a sphere; it would flicker and change four or five times each second, which is the rate at which the eyeball jumps from one fixation to another; some parts of it would be blurred and some parts of it would be in focus; it would have a blurry wedge in the corner where the nose is; there would be a blank patch near the middle for the blindspot; and so on. But explaining exactly where the train of thought goes wrong is a delicate and complicated task.

I have explored these connected ideas about perception and art and their roots in seventeenth century optics in several places, most recently in my book *The Objective Eye*. I've tried to show how our understanding of the seminal developments in Western art can be transformed by philosophy and by a philosophically informed study of the history of optics. More broadly, I've argued that a correct understanding of the realistic impulse in Western art is threatened from two sides: from one side by the misconceived ideas about vision mentioned above and from the other side by the idea that the impression of reality some works of art convey more forcibly than others depends on the novelty or the familiarity of the system of pictorial conventions the artist used to represent his subject. (Philosophers associate the latter idea with Nelson Goodman's book *Languages of Art*, but it was already well established in art history when this was published, partly because of the influence of Roman Jakobson and Leo Steinberg.) The principal aim of the last two chapters of *The Objective Eye* is to develop a way of understanding realism in art that is free from errors of both kinds.

The other main contribution I have made to the philosophical study of art concerns the idea of depiction in general. I've defended a qualified and — if I can put it this way — purified version of the so-called 'resemblance' theory of depiction: the theory that pictures differ from texts in resembling the objects that they represent. Two related mistakes led philosophers to abandon this theory. First, they mistakenly thought that resemblance is a relation, whereas the truth is that 'resembles,' 'is like,' 'looks like,' etc. can function as two-place predicates and express relations (e.g. 'SoHo is like Hampstead'); but they can also function as copular verbs, that is, as part of a one-place predicate (e.g. 'SoHo is like a village'). Second, there is a fundamental distinction between a picture's having some generic content (e.g. depicting a bearded man, or a town) and a picture's portraying an individual (e.g. depicting Jesus, or Jerusalem). All figurative pictures have some generic content, but only some portray, just as all descriptions have a sense but only some refer ('the present king of France' has a sense but does not refer). But philosophers have commonly confused or amalgamated theories about the sense of pictures and theories about their reference (e.g. Wollheim), or assumed that a theory of depiction is first and foremost a theory of reference (e.g. Goodman) — as it were, a theory of the portrait — and that a theory of sense can be developed from it, rather as Wittgenstein's theory of meaning in the *Tractatus* was developed from his conception of a name. These mistakes are related because reference is a relation whereas sense is not. So if resemblance is assumed to be a relation, the resemblance theory of depiction is bound to be interpreted as a theory of pictorial reference, whereas it is (or should be) a theory of pictorial sense.

I have argued that if we correct these mistakes, and if we appreciate that a theory of depiction is first and foremost a theory of pictorial sense, we can recover the common-sense idea that pictures depict things by copying (or, better, presenting) their form and colour. So instead of rejecting the resemblance theory, as philosophers have tended to do in the last fifty years, we can make it precise. The most recent statement of my views on this subject is in a lecture I contributed to the Royal Institute of Philosophy's 2010–11 series, Philosophy and the Arts. Finally, I would mention an article about Ramachandran's and Zeki's writings on the visual arts, 'Art and Neuroscience.' This isn't a major piece of research. I wrote it over a weekend. But it attacks an idea that is rapidly gaining currency today, that neuroscience can build new foundations for the study of the visual arts. I argue that the leading ideas in so-called neuroaesthetics are intellectually jejune and insufficiently informed about philosophy or art; and I try to show, as I did when I wrote about Renaissance perspective, that while science can sometimes correct misconceptions that arise in philosophy, the reverse is also true.

3. What is the proper role of the study of images in relation to other academic disciplines?

Philosophy is a thickly interwoven subject. If I may borrow an image from neuroscience, in spite of my comments above, questions in philosophy are almost as densely connected with each other as neurons in the brain. The philosophical study of images cannot be divorced from the philosophy of perception, the philosophy of language, philosophical logic, and other areas of philosophical enquiry. And philosophical, historical, and scientific studies of images are also closely related to each other. This is why the subject is so challenging and so rewarding. But — at least at present — the relationship between philosophy and science is the one that we need most to understand correctly, and that is most widely misunderstood. Many cognitive scientists interested in the visual arts have a very sketchy knowledge of philosophy in general and of the philosophy of art in particular. For their part, many philosophers are uncritical of ideas in cognitive science that seem to confirm their prior commitments or intuitions, and their assessment of competing ideas in the field tends to be superficial and unsystematic, if it happens at all. There is an unfortunate tendency among philosophers to equate respect for science with deference to recent scientific ideas, however speculative and however coloured with philosophical ideas they would otherwise dismiss as muddled or simplistic if they came across them in their colleagues' work. Ultimately, what is needed is a properly thought-out view of the relationship between science and philosophy in general. This is something philosophers interested in depiction need as much as philosophers of physics and philosophers of mind, because of the extensive scientific literature about the perception of pictures. But there is little evidence of it in the philosophical literature about pictorial art.

4. What do you consider the most important topics and/or contributions in the study of images?

The most important texts in the last fifty years are surely Gombrich's *Art and Illusion* and Goodman's *Languages of Art*. *Art and Illusion* may be muddled at many crucial points, but it is pathbreaking; and the principal ideas in *Languages of Art* may be utterly misguided, but they are presented with a power, economy, and panache that makes them impossible to ignore. Wollheim is an interesting writer about art, but in my view his writings on the fundamental philosophical questions about images are overrated. In particular, his theory of representation in the visual arts (which results from an insufficiently penetrating criticism of Gombrich) and his theory of realism are both superficial. Unlike Goodman's ideas, one does not learn much by engaging with them, except that they are wrong. All in all, I have probably learned more from the great philosophically-informed art historians in the German tradition (Wölfflin, Panofsky, Wind, Gombrich, etc.) than from philosophical studies of the visual arts. As for topics, I suppose it is obvious that I regard the topics I have studied as the most important ones — that is why I have studied them. The most important gap in my own work, I think, is that I have not written extensively about the connection between questions about the nature of pictorial art — or specific pictorial media, such as photography — and questions about its value as art. It is not essential to think about this in order to address the basic questions about depiction, realism, and perspective on which I have focused, any more than it is essential to think about poetry in the philosophy of language. But it is a rich field of study.

5. What are the most important open problems in this field and what are the prospects/avenues for progress?

Important problems in philosophy always remain open. As for progress, I believe it is possible. But I worry that increasing specialization stands in the way of progress because of the interconnectedness of philosophy, which I mentioned earlier. Valuable new ideas in philosophy are often the result of making unexpected connections between different parts of the subject, and specialization makes this less likely to occur. Wittgenstein made a sardonic comment about progress in philosophy: "I read 'philosophers are no nearer to the meaning of 'Reality' than Plato got...' What a singular situation. How singular then that Plato has been able to get even as far as he did! Or that we could get no further afterwards! Was it because Plato was so clever?" (*Culture and Value*: 22.) Anthony Kenny once commented that he thought this probably was the reason! Be that as it may, I think we can make progress in philosophy. But unlike in science we can also make regress. Regress in science could now only happen as a result of a social catastrophe, whereas in philosophy it can easily happen from one generation to the next, just because a certain range of philosophical literature has gone out of fashion. (Think of the decline of logic in the early modern period.) Also unlike in science, progress in philosophy does not mean adding to a body of established and agreed results. It is reasonable to hope for progress, but not consensus.

As I see it, philosophy has two complementary aims, one constructive and the other destructive. The constructive aim of philosophy is to provide a systematic exposition of the principal concepts or ideas used in a domain of thought and to modify or replace existing concepts when they give rise to paradoxes or embody confusion. In some parts of philosophy, such as ethics or philosophy of mind, the domain of thought is one we all inhabit, simply in virtue of being mature, socialized human beings; whereas in other parts of philosophy, such as philosophy of law or philosophy of physics, it is not. When it succeeds, this kind of philosophy makes us self-conscious thinkers, aware of the structure of our own systems of concepts and ideas. The destructive aim of philosophy, on the other hand, is to expose and criticize the errors and myths that dominate our thinking when this intellectually informed and self-conscious use of concepts fails. For example, in ethics, the claim that only pleasure and pain have intrinsic value; in metaphysics, the theory that space and time are created by the mind; and in psychology, the idea that thoughts and feelings are electrical activities in the brain. It was because he was so preoccupied with philosophy in its destructive mode that Wittgenstein described the philosopher's treatment of a question as being like the treatment of an illness.

In the philosophical study of images, the principal concepts include form, colour, depiction (sense), depiction (reference), realism, etc. And the myths include (i) painting is mirroring; (ii) mirror images are pictures; and (iii) vision is the result of interpreting images in the eye. If I could encourage one avenue for making progress, it would be basing the theory of images more firmly on a careful study of the concepts of colour and form, and on the distinction between an optical image and a picture.

Selected publications by John Hyman

1999. "How knowledge works." *Philosophical Quarterly*, October: 433–451.

2001. "-ings and -ers." *Ratio Special Issue: Meaning and Representation*, December: 298–317.

2003. "Pains and places." *Philosophy*, January: 5–24.

2005. "Realism and Relativism in the Theory of Art." *Proceedings of the Aristotelian Society* 105, 1: 25–53.

2005. "What, if anything, are colours relative to?" *Philosophy*, October: 475–494.

2006. "Knowledge and evidence." *Mind*, October: 633–658.

2006. *The Objective Eye: Color, Form and Reality in the Theory of Art*. Chicago: University of Chicago Press.

2010. "Art and Neuroscience." In Roman Frigg & Matthew Hunter, eds., *Beyond Mimesis and Convention: Representation in Art and Science*. Dordrecht: Springer. German: 2006. "Kunst und Neurowissenschaft." In Matthias Bauer, Fabienne Liptay, & Susanne Marschall, eds., *Kunst und Kognition*. München: Wilhelm Fink Verlag.

2010. "The Road to Larissa." *Ratio Special Issue: Agents and their Actions*, December. 393–414.

2013. "Depiction." In Anthony O'Hear, ed, *Philosophy and the Arts*. Cambridge: Cambridge University Press.

Forthcoming. "Voluntariness and Choice." *Philosophical Quarterly*.

11

Claude Imbert

Professor Emerita of Philosophy and Logic at Ecole Normale Supérieure

---

1. Why were you initially drawn to the study of images?

My initially naive interest in pictures of all sorts sprung from a double discontent. I was disappointed, even embarrassed, by the emptiness of aesthetic commentaries, expecting a kind of intrinsic knowledge that I wasn't able to specify, probably due to the vast diversity of images. Overcoming this uncertainty was my primary motivation for opening the visual domain to issues far beyond the focus on rules of depiction. The challenge was, paradoxically, to demand from images an alternative access to reality, a more roundabout but richer access that would surmount the limitations of phenomenology — themselves a legacy from the ancient Greek submission of visual to verbal expression, of the visible to the sayable. Now, within the image, a neglected or repudiated mode of knowledge had opened a space for itself between the discursive, mathematical, or immediately perceptual regimes. One that, in fact, underlies all of them. However important, images were kept at a distance, bereft of any epistemological interest and otherwise devalued. Here, Merleau-Ponty became a pioneer. After having demonstrated the untenability of Kant's account of experience, as well as the incapacity of the discursive realm to uphold a supreme standard for knowledge, he liberated himself from transcendental criticism, which denied the epistemological import of images by relegating it to the realm of taste. Haunted by the nightmare of a philosophy reduced to the emptiness of its intentionalities, he kept himself equally distanced from rampant deconstruction and historicist narrativity. His last words were devoted to the philosophical rehabilitation of painting.

2. What do you consider your contribution to the field?

Since all this was, more or less explicitly, about epistemology, I continued to develop the link that I sensed between images, in the true sense, and knowledge in two different but complementary ways.

On the one hand, taking my point of departure from what was called "mathematical logic" — somehow an antidote to phenomenology —

I thoroughly investigated the highly contested graphical notations of Gottlob Frege (1879). Now, it soon dawned on me that this *ideography* (badly named, something that in itself reveals how wrongly the question has been addressed) had been the source of all fruitful syntactic analyses as well as of the attempts at computational implementation, once it was freed from the Kantian epistemology of the object. This reference to the object was the source of the paradoxes it had suffered from in the beginning, now discovering its full epistemological import, based on its capacity of densifying information (*dichten*, which is also a poetic act, as Frege noted, see Imbert 1971). Thus, the "ideographical" representation of order, of a function, of an algebraic operation, or even the implementation of a proof by transformation and substitution imposed a distribution of symbols that rebel against predicative linearity. This paved the way for a series of diagrams capable of innervating mathematical writing. Consider, for example, the graphical transcription of a geometric proportion, a substitution matrix, and more recently, the indexation on the Gauss surface of so-called *imaginary* quantities. It is at a late stage, forty years down the line, that Frege was able to explicate the nature of his invention as a *Hilfessprache*, an auxiliary language, freed from the modes of enunciation and from the linearity of natural language. A sort of insistent connivance traversed all the graphical modes of representation, awaiting explication. The last step in my endeavor consisted in situating Frege's invention in the context of the support he received from the Zeiss Foundation (in Iena), whose research program aimed for an extension in visual form of an intelligible domain foreign to the discursive economy. His *Logical Investigations* repeatedly resort to the optical paradigm, talking about *real image* and *virtual image*. The upshot of this was a double mobilization of the graphical surface, which I did not consider an illustration, but a contender of discursive information: i.e., a construction of graphical notations on a par with diagrams, working the dimensions of the surface without reference to empirical or Euclidian space. We still do not know what will produce three-dimensionality in this domain, between the simulation of the scale model and an as yet undefined indexing capacity. As an aside: the mapping of the central nervous system now defines its basic units in terms of *voxels* (volumetric units) and no longer in *pixels*. The always called for conceptual activity is nowadays performed without necessarily being integrated into the propositional frame — or to borrow from Wittgenstein, one might say it belongs to another *logical space*. Such new encoding introduced a sort of familiarity between different domains of knowledge.

On the other hand, history of art, understood as the history of artful productions, has sought out a myriad of graphical possibilities, densifying its poetics by means of different sorts of procedures such as embedding, collage, montage, dimensions of colors, and the framing of one space within another space — all sorts of techniques which considerably enrich visual information and visual intelligence. Simultaneously, or almost simultaneously, the reflection on art has changed its methods in two ways. Philosophers gave up Kant's aesthetic enclosure, the guarantor of his transcendental phenomenology (as evidence of the machinery of the faculties and the cornerstone of his whole system, by his own admission). Here Cassirer, with his symbolic forms, or Benjamin (1936/1963) pinpointing the existence of an "expositional value" (*Ausstellungswert*) accompanied the most original research by art historians. They left it to the 'connoisseurs' to identify the artworks and the influences and instead devoted their energy to capturing the procedures (what Michael Baxandall and Svetlana Alpers (1994), in their analysis of Tiepolo, have called "pictorial intelligence"). A case in point is Victor Stoichita's (1999) work on the framing and inclusion of several images in one and the same painting. The same people who have made us acknowledge the import of dense graphisms have also remarked on the anthropological signification of non-occidental "images" — obvious references here are Franz Boas, Aby Warburg, and Claude Lévi-Strauss (cf. Imbert 2003, 2008b, 2013). Since the image allows for a great liberty of framing and explicitly uses other dimensions (for example color, to which Wittgenstein and Merleau-Ponty were as sensitive as the painters), it lent itself to anthropological research (Imbert 2008a). Testifying as any ethnographic material, the image plunged "symbolic" production into some shared and basic cognitive performances, associating the nature of human vision with the local, indirect, and opaque negotiations through which a society adapts it manners of living to the configuration of its surroundings. If Merleau-Ponty's generation had thus pinpointed the limitations of the strategies aiming at making language and vision converge — and demonstrated the impossibility of enriching a phenomenological tradition already saturated by its own constraints — it was still necessary to display the positive side of this liberation. Contributions to this project are what Michel Foucault called "the right of images" (Imbert 2004), what Gilles Deleuze called the "logic of sensation," and what Aby Warburg, calling attention to a blind spot in the philosophy of Enlightenment, invoked with one of his provocative expressions (the composite density of which may have hampered its comprehension): "the human rights of the eye."

This blind spot is patent even in the diagrammatic essays in the *Encyclopédie,* intended to cure it, or in David's first paintings. They are all closer to being characterizations of objects or plots than *sui generis* pictorial distribution — such as the paintings by Delacroix after the aquarelles executed on motifs from Morocco.

3. What is the proper role of the study of images in relation to other academic disciplines?

I can only give a preliminary answer to this question, but I do think it touches something essential: an image, in the most general conception of the term, is not a representation of things or bodies, it is the simultaneous handling and invention of information within a symbolic regime, following or forcing the education of the visual field in accordance with an innovative syntax — that is to say an unprecedented mobilization and articulation of visual tracks. Baudelaire's actuality resides in this point, and through him, that of the anonymous and composite figure of "the painter of modern life," cumulating in the figures of Delacroix and Manet. The anonymous Monsieur G. contributed as a journalist and reporter for the London magazine *Illustrated News*, where he performed an inscription of glances (and not of things or stories), enforcing the discursive graph of information. As to Baudelaire, he dispersed in his "petits poèmes en prose" (little prose poems), snapshots of emotion to the same effect. In this way, the theory of images would take up from the anthropology of the contemporary world, in its incessant trial of modernity. It also explores a wide fanning out of unexplored possibilities in the history of art as well as in the history of geometries and diagrams.

As a consequence, all disciplines are concerned by the possible or explicit use of figures and images in a domain where the cognitive sciences enter into symbiosis with the pragmatics of gesture and enunciation. The knowledge about images, which may concern the more or less foreseeable innovations within this medium, is in fact an ever-disputable element of a process of survival by means of intellectual, cultural, and scientific enrichment. At a European scale, where this incessant process of modernity was originally defined, the issue is indistinguishably historical and anthropological. This is an essential point for any philosophy: long concerned with the categorization of what is seen, the characterization of things, the criterion for existence and for the legitimizing of the real, it needs to take into account the indirect ways in which information and the foliage of intermediary and interchangeable spaces work in order to uphold a realism that urban modernity has populated with artifacts. This would be in accordance with an epistemological hypothesis that I have developed elsewhere (Imbert 2010–2011): *There is no intelligence before the production of the intelligible*, that is to say the displaying of explicit dimensions and the soliciting of our cognitive resources, including primarily those of the visual field. Wittgenstein said that a grammar provides sufficient dimensions; today one is more likely to say that the configuration of an image, the syntax deployed on a surface or in space, offers thought a wealth of possible ramifications.

The structure of a sponge, an archipelago distribution, a bottle drainer, harbor more intelligence than an Aristotelian tree (Bredekamp 2005, Imbert 2008a). The same also goes for the syntax of Proust or Joyce, or for the syntax of Frege and for those who, like Gödel, appreciated its relevance. They all lead to products that are difficult, or impossible, to *speak*, but that can be read and are amenable to variations. The stakes are enrichment and survival. The common world is not merely a social product; to experiment requires much more than just a theory of decision and its criterions.

4. What do you consider the most important topics and/or contributions in the study of images? and 5. What are the most important open problems in this field and what are the prospects/ avenues for progress?

From this point of view, your two last questions coincide. The most important contributions have been by anthropologists, starting from Boas, Warburg and Lévi-Strauss. In France, several eminent scholars and institutions (see, for example, the research departments now associated with museums) work on the most multifarious forms of symbolism, testifying to a recent reassessment devoted to diagrams, machines, and automats, considered for their intervention into a visual field always in the process of acculturation. This work renews the topology of images, which also implies urbanism, design, and, along with that, robotics and architecture. This investigation also integrates the graphical investment of walls, surfaces, whether woven or modeled, fabric, and ritual objects — and all this on a huge time scale. This praxis, highlighted by anthropologists (Leroi-Gourhan (1964–1965), Lévi-Strauss (1964–1971), testifies to the symbolic anthropization of gesturality: a ruse of hominization, a strategy that prefers the extension of the visual field intercepted by a surface, the advantage of the gaze and of its emotion, on or for the predatory grasp, this disposition of the hunter/gatherer that contemporary humans assume as their ancestor.

One of most important topics to investigate is the gestural investment of the body in symbols, games, performances, and choreographies. All of these exemplify a modification of the visual strategy in the long-term, incessant *process of modernity*, which has nothing to do with neither a passive adaptation nor with the gross Cartesianism to which it is opposed. We are here dealing with local operations and inventions that explore ways of negotiating with reality, which originated in urban life and today in an emerging ecology. In this sense, and leaning on Baudelaire and Warburg, one must identify the different ways in which the image and its unexpected variations are substitutes for the sacrificial conjuration, insisting on the continuous historical reconfiguration of a shared visual space, as well as scientific diagrams, mathematical compact writings, machine-languages used in computing and the expansion of artistic production in landscapes, gardens, and public squares.

It is important to examine how a human visual field is constituted, trained, and transformed, how it functions as an archive and thus establishes itself as one of the surest ways of investigating the unknown. As Merleau-Ponty said: "The painter throws away the fish and keeps the net" (1969: 66) — a metaphor which today could be enriched in accordance with all the possible senses of net: web, structure, configuration, chromatic grid, musical score, topology of bifurcations, fissures or fractals, and geographies. Such conditions for a possible analysis of the image as prolepsis and structuring configuration implies renouncing the "subject–object" perspective and the postulate of representational accuracy. It is the price to be paid to seize a way of exploration and of anticipation proper to the image and graphisms within which their poetic is already placed. Is it possible to deny or neglect a resource that is both actual and urgent while at the same time deeply rooted in anthropological archeology? Picasso did seize its permanence rather well: painting, he said, is simultaneously apotropaic[1] and propitiatory.[2] Such a conjuration of the informal and the invisible fuels the philosophers' interest in the image, but also the vocation of painters, or designers. All together they shape new possibilities, from the scale model, the diagram, the simulation, the emulation now basic processes in digital thinking, to those logical or 'literary' spaces that I have identified as a liberation from propositional constraint and the unfolding of a graphical intelligence (to retain here the meaning of the Greek term *graphé*, which means at once drawing, inscription, image, and writing). Today, architecture conceives itself as mediating the interior configuration of the public, civil, and urban space. This virtual integration of images anticipates, sums up, and accomplishes a social integration that amounts to life forms, what I elsewhere have called the "coinage of the visible" ("la monnaie du regard," Imbert 2010–2011).

Bibliography

Baxandall, Michael & Svetlana Alpers. 1994. *Tiepolo and the Pictorial Intelligence*. New Haven: Yale University Press.

Benjamin, Walter. 1936/1963. "Das Kunstwerk im Zeitalter seiner technischen Reproduzierbarkeit." In *Das Kunstwerk im Zeitalter seiner technischen Reproduzierbarkeit: Drei Studien zur Kunstsoziologie*. Frankfurt: Suhrkamp.

---

[1] Intended to ward off evil.

[2] Intended to appease or conciliate.

Bredekamp, Horst. 2005. *Darwins Korallen: Die frühen Evolutionsdiagramme und die Tradition der Naturgeschichte*. Berlin: Wagenbach.

Frege, Gottlob. 1879. *Begriffsschrift: eine der arithmetischen nachgebildete Formelsprache des reinen Denkens*. Halle: Verlag von Louis Nebert.

Leroi-Gourhan, André. 1964–1965. *Le geste et la parole*, vols. 1–2. Paris: Albin Michel.

Lévi-Strauss, Claude. 1964–1971. *Mythologiques*, vols. 1–4. Paris: Plon.

Merleau-Ponty, Maurice. 1969. *La prose du monde*. Paris: Gallimard.

Stoichita,Victor. 1999. *L'instauration du tableau: métapeinture à l'aube des temps modernes*. Geneva: Droz.

Selected publications by Claude Imbert

1971. Translation and introduction to Écrits logiques et philosophiques: Gottlob Frege. Paris: Seuil.

2003. "Warburg, de Kant à Boas." *L'Homme* 165: 11–40.

2004. "Les droits de l'image." In Michel Foucault, *La Peinture de Manet*. Paris: Seuil.

2008a. "Le bleu de la mer années 1950." In Emmanuel de Saint Aubert, ed., *Maurice Merleau-Ponty*. Paris: Hermann.

2008b. *Lévi-Strauss le passage du Nord-Ouest*. Paris: Herne.

2010–2011. "La monnaie du regard." *La Part de l'œil* 25, 26.

2013. "Boas, de Berlin à New York, manières de vivre, manières de voir." In Michel Espagne & Isabelle Kalinowski, eds., *Franz Boas: Le travail du regard*. Paris: Colin.

12

Martin Jay

Professor of History at the University of California, Berkeley

---

1. Why were you initially drawn to the study of images?

There is always an over-determined and ultimately inexplicable set of reasons that impels anyone to move towards one area of interest as opposed to another. My father, who was an advertising executive, had a talent for drawing, and even exhibited some of his work before I was born. My daughters became interested in visual culture at about the same time as I did; one now teaches art history at the Fashion Institute of Technology in New York, the other is a photographer with an MFA from the School of Visual Arts. So to a certain extent, I have been immersed in a familial context in which visual issues more than, say, musical ones were paramount. But my own professional interest really came through the discursive backdoor. That is, I first systematically began to think about visual issues when I became aware of the anti-ocularcentric discourse in France whose contours I tried to trace in *Downcast Eyes: The Denigration of Vision in Twentieth-Century French Thought* (1993), a book for which I began to do research around 1983. Inevitably, the object of that discourse became itself of importance to me, so I began to spend more time looking at and thinking about visual phenomena. But I still proudly retain my amateur, autodidactic status when it comes to the serious analysis of images — and I am always very much aware of my limitations in comparison to colleagues who have been rigorously trained in art history, cinema studies, the history of photography, new media, the science of vision, etc.

2. What do you consider your contribution to the field?

As an intellectual historian, I have tried to map out the territories on which visual practices and the theories about them have intersected. I've been willing to venture generalizations about, say, scopic regimes or anti-ocularcentric discourses that scholars more deeply rooted in specific locations on that map might have missed or felt uncomfortable proposing. As an outsider to the settled disciplinary fields focusing on visual phenomena, I've been freer to transgress boundaries that may limit their horizons.

If I had to confess what makes me proudest, however, it would be that some of my writing seems to have stimulated the actual work done by practicing artists, who find in it a way to situate their creative impulses in a larger context of meaning. Contemporary visual artists, in my experience, can be very sophisticated about the theoretical issues that exercise academics. They often, of course, resist being reduced to exemplars of categories — Barnet Newman's famous quip about the difference between birds and ornithologists will be recalled — but at other times, they are grateful for a discursive framework that helps orient their individual creations.

3. What is the proper role of the study of images in relation to other academic disciplines?

I am very reluctant to legislate what is proper and what isn't, especially when it comes to the practices of other disciplines besides my own (and I'm not comfortable doing it there either). Some disciplines use images as evidentiary documents providing a window to the world; others examine the ways in which images construct imaginary or ideological worlds of their own. Some isolate images and seek to understand them in terms of immanent traditions of image-making and image-reception; others integrate them into larger contexts of meaning and production. Some disciplines examine the cultural discourses that intersect with and help us interpret images; others stress the physiology of sight and draw on scientific advances to explain the way vision works. In short, images are at the cross-section of many different approaches and help us to address many different kinds of questions. No one should limit or privilege one over the other.

4. What do you consider the most important topics and/or contributions in the study of images?

Let me answer this question with a series of questions of my own, which situate the study of images in the larger context of the senses as a whole: How has the general sensorium been discursively differentiated in various contexts? Have all cultures posited the same five senses or have others been included? If, as some scientists have claimed, there are no fewer than seventeen ways in which animals actually sense the world, have some beyond the canonical five been attributed to humans as well? When have putative sixth senses like balance, desire, or even speech been added to the mix? How has the role of proprioception, the kinaesthetic sense, been understood? Is there a primal "inner touch" that tells us we are sentient creatures, and if so, does it have a history? Can perception be "extrasensory?" Or rather, to put it in historical terms, what attempts have been made to identify ESP and how have they been received?

Have all cultures ranked the senses hierarchically in the ways that most commentators in the West have done since the Greeks with the distancing senses of vision and hearing supposedly "nobler" than the other, more proximate three? Have some cultures developed different hierarchies, perhaps experiential as well as discursive, that have been transformed historically? Is the differentiation and uneven development of the senses, however many we may posit, legislated by nature or the product of historical forces? When, if ever, does the prevalent "ocularcentrism" of so many cultures cede pride of place to other senses? Can one locate "audiocentric" or "tactocentric" cultures, let alone "gastrocentric" or "olfactocentric" ones? Has the process of differentiation and ranking ever been reversed, letting intersensorial dedifferentiation occur instead? Is synaesthesia, the harmonious integration of the senses, a genuine paradise lost or merely a fantasy of poetic imagination?

How has culture developed technologies to extend and enhance the senses, creating an "exosomatic" array of devices that compensate for the limits of our creaturely nature? In addition to obvious examples, such as the armor and anesthesia that protects our vulnerable touch, the telescopes and microscopes that extend our visual range, and the listening devices that detect sound frequencies our ears cannot register or microphones that magnify the volume of our voices, what other prosthetic devices have transformed our natural capacities? How has the relationship between temporality and sensuality been historically affected with the invention of devices — extending as far back as written language itself — to sustain, transmit, and reproduce sensual experiences, ranging from the fixing chemicals of the perfumer to the digital cameras and sound recorders that have so transformed the visual and aural sensescapes of the modern world? Have some senses been effected more than others by these technological extensions, allowing, for example, a more explicit distinction between nature and culture such as that indicated by the now familiar contrast between "vision and visuality?" What about those techniques and inventions designed to dull the senses — even to suspend their effects temporarily — ranging from the ascetic practices of fakirs able to walk on hot coals to the miracles of modern medical anaesthesia? Can there be a disentanglement of sense data from the actual human sensorium, leading to an independent realm of impersonal sensual experience in what has been called "the culture of diagram" (Bender and Marrinan 2010)?

How has the loss or impairment of the senses been understood, lamented, and alleviated historically? Is, for example, the British novelist David Lodge right in saying that "deafness is comic, as blindness is tragic?" Is the rubric of "disability studies" the best category to use in interpreting reactions to sensual deprivation or modification? Might the loss of one sense have enhanced the acuity of another, thus paradoxically producing a new "enability?" What of the claims for a separate but in no way inferior "deaf culture" that has generated an extensive literature of its own, some of it historical? How do we understand the relationship, if any, between the deliberate elimination of collective sensual experiences — say the allegedly "foul" smells of traditional life eradicated in the name of hygiene — and physiological conditions such as the personal loss of smell scientists called anosmia? Have there been radical impairments — or perhaps better put as "de-skillings" — of the senses in certain cultures, as Theodor W. Adorno provocatively argued was the case with the "regression of listening" in modern audiences of music? Is the artificial stimulation, manipulation, and maybe even derangement of the senses also an issue worth studying in a late capitalism that operates through the relentless instigation of new consumer demand?

How can we plausibly periodize and narrate changes in the sensorium in different contexts? Do the periods we posit easily map on to others familiar to us from political, economic, technological, or social history? Or do they follow their own internal development? As the field of sensory history has matured, have grosser, bolder generalizations about entire epochs faded in plausibility? What is the relationship between hegemonic cultural assumptions about the senses — call them, if you will, a period's sensory *mentalité* — and the actual material and corporeal practices of the era, which may vary according to social, economic, and gender differences? Even attempts to delineate more modestly circumscribed "scopic or auditory regimes" have had to face criticisms that they fail to account for evidence that undermines their putative homogeneity. Similarly, grand narratives in which one dominant sense is replaced by another in an epochal shift have been increasingly called into question. If, for example, Sigmund Freud was right in arguing in a famous footnote in *Civilization and its Discontents* (1962) that with the adoption of an erect posture, hominids left behind the priority of olfactory stimulation in favor of visual ones, then why, one wonders, did the same replacement have to occur again with the onset of the modern age?

5. What are the most important open problems in this field and what are the prospects/avenues for progress?

I would only add to the previous answer by saying that it might be productive to focus on the dialectic of embeddedness and disembeddedness that isolates vision and reintegrates it with the sensorium in general. Is this relationship naturally or historically determined, and if so, what are its variations?

Bibliography

Bender, John & Michael Marrinan. 2010. *The Culture of Diagram.* Stanford, Calif.: Stanford University Press.

Freud, Sigmund. 1930/1962. *Civilization and its Discontents.* James Strachey, trans. & ed. New York: Norton.

Selected publications by Martin Jay

1993a. *Force Fields: Between Intellectual History and Cultural Critique.* New York & London: Routledge.

1993b. *Downcast Eves: The Denigration of Vision in Twentieth-Century French Thought.* Berkeley: University of California Press.

1996. Editor with Teresa Brennan. *Vision in Context: Historical and Contemporary Perspectives on Sight.* New York: Routledge.

2003. *Refractions of Violence.* New York: Routledge.

2005. "The Current State of Visual Culture Studies." *Journal of Visual Culture* 4, 2.

2009/2010. "Magical Nominalism: Photography and the Re-enchantment of the World." *Culture, Theory and Critique* 50, 2–3: 16–183. Reprinted in Neal Curtis, ed., *The Pictorial Turn.* Abingdon: Routledge.

2011. *Essays from the Edge: Parerga and Paralipomena.* Charlottesville: University of Virginia Press.

13

John M. Kennedy

Professor of Psychology at the University of Toronto

---

1. Why were you initially drawn to the study of images?

I was "drawn" to the study of images, and drew conclusions!

I read voluminously as a child, loved drawing and liked the Belfast Museum and Art Gallery, especially touring exhibitions. I read an encyclopedia of art as a boy. I drew a lot and I vividly remember Mr. Johnson at Rosetta Primary School holding up my picture of a river for general admiration. Mr. Rowlands at my public "grammar" school, Royal Belfast Academical Institution ("Inst"), ordered a copy to be painted of one of my pictures. I have quite forgotten the names of the two art teachers who held up my pictures for ridicule! Another teacher whose name conveniently slips my mind wanted me to stop drawing all over my textbooks. At Inst, I decided to become a psychologist and, in my second year at Queen's University Belfast, I came of the opinion that to understand psychology we have to understand perception. I read Donald Olding Hebb that year and I took seriously his advocacy of perceptual learning and his assumption that Edgar Rubin's figure-ground phenomenon was basic to perception.

Figure-ground occurs when a line or contour between two fields is seen as shaping one of the fields. The shape is the figure, and it appears as foreground. The other field is background, and appears to continue behind the foreground. Sometimes the background is empty (as for the middle arrow on the left in Figure 1). This is the standard Rubin figure-ground case. Sometimes the background is a clear surface (as in the lowest arrow on the left in Figure 1). As a graduate student at Cornell I realized figure-ground was only one possibility at a border. Figure-figure occurs at the corner of a room or cube formed by two surfaces meeting (as in the rightmost arrow in Figure 1), since both of the surfaces meeting at the corner are foreground. What are the possible arrangements of foreground and background, I asked, and which do lines or contours depict? This last question can be put as "what can a line depict?" To my surprise, I found no one had asked this question — no psychologist, art historian, anthropologist, nor philosopher. I set to work.

Besides figure-ground and figure-figure, lines can depict wires (as in the top left arrow in Figure 1). These are ground-figure-ground, for the wire is the foreground. The wire can have a definite background surface like the top of the cube, or empty background like the top part of the wire-line. Depicting a crack, the line stands for the background, recessed behind the two surfaces on either side of the crack (as in the middle bottom arrow in Figure 1). An interesting case I realized a few years ago during my time at Wissenschaftskolleg zu Berlin is the kind of corner made when an object such as a cube sits on a table (bottom left arrow in Figure 1). The tabletop surface and the cube front surface meet at the corner, and both are foreground. But the tabletop foreground surface continues under the cube. That is, a foreground surface continues at the corner, behind the common border. The only surface combination that is impossible is ground-ground. Though two foregrounds can meet at a corner, to have a background there has to be a foreground.

Figure 1 shows the possibilities of outline. If the picture used uniform solid colour areas, it would have a contour in the place of each line. It would be a contour picture, not outline. Figure-ground edges and figure-figure corners and to a limited extent figure-ground-figure cracks could still be shown. To create a contour picture, all that needs to be done is to darken (fill-in) the region on one side of the line. But the wire-line could not be shown. Darken the region on one side of the line and one of the wire's borders would disappear. At the line showing a crack, the width of the crack is shown in Figure 1, but if the region to one side is darkened the two surfaces coming close to form a crack would be depicted as flush. The picture would have the same shape if it were showing one surface was stained.

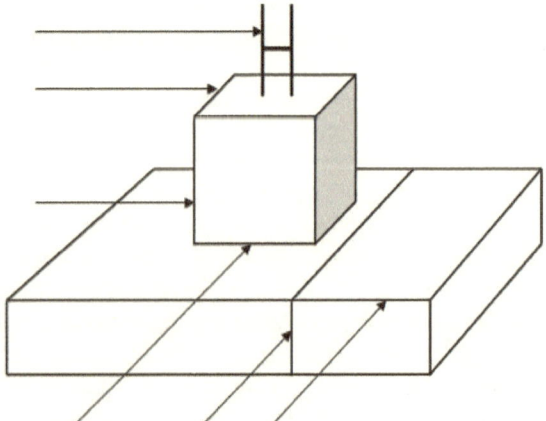

Figure 1. Each arrow points to a different figure-ground option.

The basic phenomena of perception of the environment have to do with the possibilities of surface perception. To understand that, one needs to describe an environment in which perception is possible, meaning that the environment provides information about its surfaces. As a result, depiction is possible because the information for a scene made of surfaces can be provided artificially, independently of the original scene, from a surface that has been suitably treated.

2. What do you consider your contribution to the field?

If depiction is possible, then perception cannot be infinitely ambiguous, despite what Berkeley and his followers argued. He said that any array of light could have an infinite number of origins. My contribution to the field, if we trace this back to my PhD thesis, begins when I showed that the problem of induction, as stated from Berkeley to Helmholtz to Goodman, is merely a tautology. It is this: "If we set no restrictions on the influences on light, then there are no restrictions on the influences on light." That established, I followed the prescription of my great doctoral supervisor James J. Gibson — I described an environment that has laws. The laws I argued for were laws about surfaces and the light from them. The natural environment has a few kinds of surface arrangements, whether we are talking about County Down or the Earth or the moon or Mars, for example. The surfaces in nature are textured. Illuminated, they can be viewed, given suitable media around the surfaces. They are tangible. An observer's vantage point lies in a set of directions to the surfaces around the vantage point. We look out and reach out from these vantage points. At vantage points, we are subject to patterned light from the surfaces, and the surfaces offer patterns of resistance to touch. The patterns are specific to the few kinds of surface arrangements we can observe in Figure 1. From the few kinds, an infinite variety can be built, in principle just like Lego blocks constructing model cities. In this environment of patterns specific to surface arrangements, perception is possible.

How specific is light in our environment? Is light unendingly and inevitably ambiguous and illusory (Kennedy et al. 1992)? Here is a useful, telling "thought demonstration:" imagine you are in a lecture room, with say 30 to 100 students. You take a picture of the students. Could you replicate that picture anywhere else in your college? Your town? Your country? The world? The answer is no, of course. Indeed, you could not replicate it anywhere in the solar system. Or, I believe, the galaxy. Conclusion? Light is specific to its sources. Pictures can capture that specificity. Light from natural surfaces is lawful, and hence specific and hence informative.

In my thesis, I described the kinds of surface edges to be perceived and I showed they could be depicted in outline drawings (Figure 1). The surface-edge principles of outline I laid out were the ones used by cave artists, I found with Judy Silver (Kennedy 1993). The examples of line depiction of surface edges that I presented are recognized universally — for example, by people from a non-pictorial culture, as I discovered with Abraham Ross (Kennedy 1993).

In my book on drawing (Kennedy 1993), I showed that shadow borders cannot be depicted in outline drawings. That is, line stands for surface edges, not all possible visual borders. And not purely visual ones like borders of shadows in particular. Continuous black lines have negative borders (like photographic negatives) as well as positive ones, like shadow borders. The negative borders make it impossible for vision to use the positive ones for shape-from-shadow perception, I found with Juan Bai (Kennedy and Bai 2004).

Surface edges project several different kinds of visual borders, it should be noted. They can be defined by combinations of luminance and spectral differences — brightness and colour borders, loosely speaking. They can be monocular or purely binocular. Purely binocular borders were popular entertainment in books in the 1990s, based on a geometry devised by Christopher Tyler. They can also be static or purely kinetic. A purely kinetic one is similar to the clear borders visible when a speckled thrush is all-but-invisible when it is sitting still on a sun-dappled patch of leaves on the ground, but as soon as it moves its borders become sharply etched. In principle, purely kinetic borders could be used to support purely binocular borders, but no one has ever devised such stimuli. Anyone want to work with me on this?

All the ways of showing surfaces and their borders, I conjecture, use outline to depict surface borders. But also, I suggest, only luminance borders can trigger shape-from-shadow perception.

Since outline shows surface edges and surface edges can be touched as well as seen, I hypothesized outline would work in touch as it does in vision — namely to show surface edges — for blind adults and children (D'Angiulli, Kennedy, & Heller 1998). This is a thoroughgoing spin on the centuries-old debate about common features of spheres and cubes in vision and touch — the "Molyneux question." Indeed, pictures do make sense to the sighted and the blind, I found in my work at Harvard, after earning my Cornell PhD with Gibson. The evidence I gathered with raised line drawing kits and the congenitally blind in many countries supports this hypothesis. This evidence is summarized in my book on drawing, written in my time at Toronto, as well as in subsequent papers that focus on notable, truly significant blind individuals — especially Gaia, a girl from Rome (Kennedy 2003), Esref, a man from Ankara

(Kennedy & Juricevic 2006a, 2006b), and Eriko, a Japanese woman now living in Augsburg (Kennedy 2009). I will always be deeply grateful to these individuals and to the insightful and important people who put us in touch, Paola Di Giulio (Italy), Joan Eroncel (Turkey) and Elke Zollitsch (Germany).

In touch as in vision, since surfaces are perceived from a vantage point, perspective is relevant to both senses. Perspective is the geometry for directions from a vantage point, and whether we look out or reach out from vantage points, we discover the directions of surface features (Kennedy & Juricevic 2006c). Hence the development of perspective drawing in blind children should be much like that in sighted children (Nicholls & Kennedy 1992). Again, the evidence is in favour of this hypothesis (Kennedy 1993). People who draw a great deal come to draw the perspective projections of objects and scenes as in Figure 2, a drawing of a cube balanced on the point by Esref, a congenitally totally blind man who makes pictures pretty much daily (Kennedy and Juricevic 2006a).

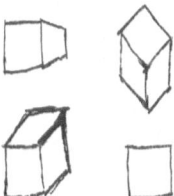

Figure 2. Drawing of a cube balanced on a point, by Esref, a congenitally, totally blind man. From Kennedy & Juricevic 2006a. By permission of Pion Press.

Apt violations of language rules create metaphors (Liu & Kennedy 1997; Kennedy & Merkas 2000; Roncero et al. 2006). Apt violations of principles of pictorial representation should create metaphoric pictures. Since vision and touch use the same principles of surface perception and depiction, this should apply to the blind as well as the sighted. I find it does — Figure 3 shows lines standing for heat and thoughts and sighs, metaphorically (Kennedy 2009). These kinds of lines were first devised, I have argued, by Bewick in Northern England in 1810 (Kennedy 1993 and 2009). Since then these "comic book devices" have spread like wildfire around the world. They have some features in common with their referent but use outline, whose "literal" use is for surface edges. Since the terms literal and metaphoric are defined with respect to language, their application to pictures is metaphoric, I must caution.

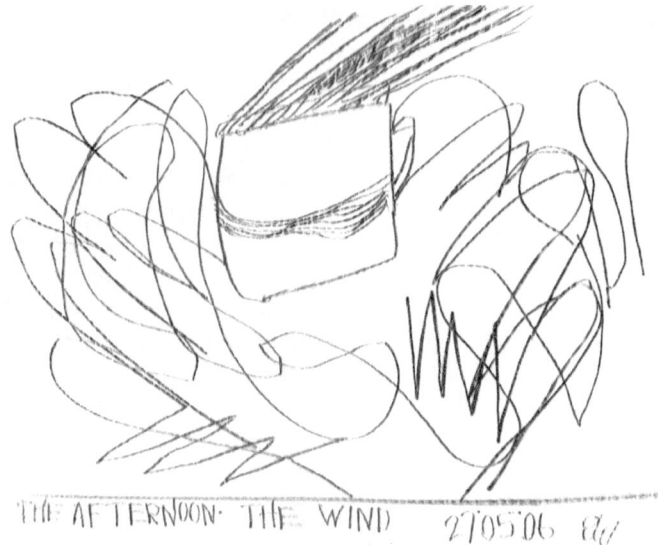

Figure 3. The afternoon, the wind, May 27 2006, by Eriko (EW). The lines around the cup stand for thoughts and the bottom middle zigzags for sighs. From Kennedy (2009). By permission of Pion Press.

3. What is the proper role of the study of images in relation to other academic disciplines?

Pictures have many, many proper uses, from advertising and play to exposing the truth of a matter as well as many proper roles in art history, biology, astronomy and other disciplines — but surely the deepest and likely the most enlightening question is this: What do they permit qua pictures? What does their very existence reveal? Make possible?

Pictures are both perceptual and representational, so on the one hand, to understand pictures, we need to understand how perception is possible. As representations, artifices based on the laws of perceptual information, they allow us to test theses about cognition and realism. That is, how do we come to perceive the world accurately? By requiring proposals about knowing, pictures do a service to philosophy. By requiring that there be an environment that can be known, they provide a basis for a psychology of sentient creatures. By requiring that pictures are artifices, they require a sentient creature that can intentionally act in the environment to represent a scene.

In practice, pictures can show parts of the world we have seen, and we see the depiction is a faithful rendering, and so when they show landscapes we have never seen directly, we can appreciate the portrayal may be accurate. Further, since they are artifices, they can include obvious violations of realism in their content, such as showing elephants cavorting on the moon, so we know they are creatures of invention and can be used to lie.

4. What do you consider the most important topics and/or contributions in the study of images?

The most important topics in the study of images come in several kinds.

Notably, to have a consistent theory of picture perception, we have to discover why perception responds to surface edges, continuous lines and dotted lines in the same way, so one can depict the other. Indeed, having this response in common is what makes depiction possible, I argue. Most relevant here is that Gestaltists like Max Wertheimer described Gestalt grouping in perception but failed to give us a perceptual mechanism that makes the common response possible. For example, notice that the set of dots . . . . . . can seem to be a unit (can seem to group together). Wertheimer noted influences such as proximity that make 5 dots plus a gap plus another 5 dots group as two units, as in . . . . But what is the mechanism in perception that produces the grouping? Wertheimer did not ask the question and so he did not attempt an answer.

We have to work out how perception responds to perspective features, e.g. convergence and eccentricity. Perspective on a landscape with a ground plane allows perception of size, distance and shape. However, perception is inexact. Foreshortening of tiles in a picture of a piazza occurs in azimuth (x dimensions) and elevation (z dimensions). The z dimensions foreshorten especially quickly. Perception treats the swift foreshortening as the tile becoming stubby.

In depiction, 2D features on the picture's surface stand for 3D features in the pictured world. The more prominent the picture surface the flatter the 3D world and, conversely, the more the 3D world is compelling the more the 2D features are seen as biased towards their 3D referent, I showed with Sherief Hammad (Hammad et al. 2008). These are perspective, pictured-world and picture-surface biases and illusions, only now being understood (Kennedy & Juricevic 2006).

Metaphors in language sometimes fail: "He had a heart of stone, though she had a heart of wheat." The stone reference works but "wheat" does not. Similarly, a picture of Pinocchio's long nose on a despot has a clear significance but what would a large Adam's apple or big toe mean? Further, in language "God is three in one" has a nice ring, but a picture of three heads emerging from one body is gauche. Which metaphors work in pictures and why is an important problem. In general all the types of tropes can be made to work in pictures, but some specific metaphors fail.

5. What are the most important open problems in this field and what are the prospects/avenues for progress?

Each field of application for pictures will define "importance" with respect to its goals. But if our concern is for the very definition of "a picture," then it is puzzles that arise for all pictures that deserve a mention here.

Why do dotted and continuous lines show continuous edges? I believe key parts of the answer will come from neuroscience. That is, mechanisms to do with the receptors and the neurones in the senses will be shown to respond equally to surface edges, continuous lines, and dots. Here is a simple or clockwork version of what will be discovered, I suggest (Kennedy et al., 2011): Regions on the sensory surface A have receptors R in regions that are roughly circular. The circles are surrounded by a ring of other receptors. The arrangement is "centre & surround" (Figure 4). All the receptors R are connected to a neurone cell C– some distance in from the sensory surface. If all the receptors are stimulated equally, the neurone C– fires only at its resting rate. But if the centre receptors R-centre are not stimulated because a black dot is in front of the centre, the surround receptors R-surround dominate the internal neurone cell C– and it deviates from its resting rate, meaning it fires a great deal.

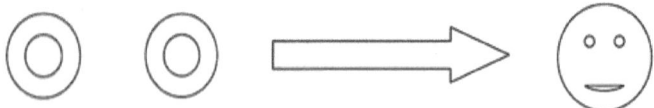

Figure 4. Two C– cell centre-surround fields (left) on the sensory surface are required to trigger a C+ cell (right) deeper in the sensory system.

Besides C–, there is another neurone cell C+ further into the interior of the sense. C– is connected to C+. So too is another C– in the vicinity of C–. The other C– cell has centre-surround R influences, and its R cells are near the first C– receptor cells. It happens that two C– cells have to be firing before C+ will deviate from its resting rate, that is, before it will fire. Hence, C+ is triggered by a pair of dots.

Of special interest is that centre-surrounds can be partially covered by a continuous line. It might be wide enough to just cover their centres, but if so, it is not entirely covering their surrounds. Hence C– cells will fire, and so too will C+. This means C+ is firing to a line as it does to dots. (This explains why lines that have two contours represent surface edges that have only one border. Both the lines and the edges trigger the same C– centre-surround cells.)

Of further interest is that a continuous surface edge can be in front of the centre-surround R fields, and the surface can cover all of the centres and part of the surrounds, but not all. The edge of the surface runs across the Rs. The edge is a chord of the centre-surround circular field. A fraction of the Rs are not covered by the surface. Hence the surface triggers the C– cells and they in turn trigger the C+ cells. Ergo, the surface edge, the continuous line and the dotted line all trigger the C+ cell.

The mechanism proposed here is best understood simply as a way of making the problem clear. The goal is to find the set of triggers that have the same result. By the definition of a perceptual representation, this is what makes depiction possible. Artificial elements trigger what is normally activated by a natural feature of the environment.

Even if dots and surface edges have a common effect in the senses, why would the perceptual result be that a dotted line depicts a continuous edge but a continuous edge does not depict a dotted line? Why the asymmetry? One reason is that both trigger a continuous function much like $y = ax + b$. But a continuous edge does not suggest a particular set of dots, fiat aside.

A 2D pictorial surface has features that depict 3D forms. One puzzle with broad implications is that the senses do not keep the information for the 2D and the 3D separate. They influence each other. In Figure 2, the top quadrilateral is seen as having four right angles. This is a "picture-surface illusion." In point of fact, the left and right angles are acute and the top and bottom angles are about 20 degrees larger and obtuse. Perception should not mix different sources of information, but it does, producing erroneous results. A task for the future is a theory predicting the size of the error.

It is one thing to argue that light from the law-governed natural surfaces of our environment is lawful, specific, and hence informative. It is another to establish what and how much needs to be present before elements on a picture surface can do the work of depiction. A single line is just that — and what it can depict is any of the options in Figure 1. As part of a Y shape, in the front vertex of the cube in Figure 1, it would still be just a potential depiction, if it were on its own. Given the arrowheads and L vertices of the cube depiction in Figure 1, it acts to show a particular surface layout. But *how many* of the arrowheads and L vertices are required before the line is so precise in function? At present, analyses of pictures are descriptions of what they can do, and it will be some time before it is clear what they need to become specific.

Bibliography

Hebb, Donald O. 1949. *The Organization of Behavior: A Neuropsychological Theory*. New York: Wiley and Sons.

Selected publications by John M. Kennedy

With Christopher D. Green, Andrea Nicholls, & Chang Hong Liu. 1992a. "Illusions and knowing what is real." *Ecological Psychology* 4, 3: 153–172.

With Andrea Nicholls. 1992b. "Drawing development: From similarity of features to direction." *Child Development* 63, 1: 227–241.

1993. *Drawing and the Blind: Pictures to Touch.* New Haven: Yale University Press.

With Chang Hong Liu. 1997. "Form symbolism, analogy and metaphor." *Psychonomic Bulletin & Review* 4, 4: 546–551.

With Amedeo D'Angiulli & Morton A. Heller. 1998. "Blind children recognizing tactile pictures respond like sighted children given guidance in exploration." *Scandinavian Journal of Psychology* 39, 3: 189–190.

With Cynthia E. Merkas. 2000. "Depictions of motion devised by a blind person." *Psychonomic Bulletin and Review* 7, 4: 700–706.

2003. "Drawings from Gaia, a blind girl." *Perception* 32, 3: 321–340.

With Juan Bai. 2004. "Line at shape-from-shadow border tested with stereo." *Perception* 33, 6: 653–665.

With Carlos Roncero & Ron Smyth. 2006a. "Similes on the internet have explanations." *Psychonomic Bulletin and Review* 13, 1: 74–77.

With Igor Juricevic. 2006b. "Foreshortening, convergence and drawings from a blind adult." *Perception* 35, 6: 847–851.

With Igor Juricevic. 2006c. "Blind man draws using diminution in three dimensions." *Psychonomic Bulletin and Review* 13, 3: 506–509.

With Igor Juricevic. 2006d. "Looking at perspective pictures from too far, too close and just right." *Journal of Experimental Psychology: General* 135, 3: 448–461.

With Sherif Hammad, Igor Juricevic, & Shazma Rajani. 2008. "Angle illusion on a picture's surface." *Spatial Vision* 21, 3–5: 451–462.

2009. "Outline, Mental States and Drawings by a Blind Woman." *Perception* 38, 10: 1481–1496.

With Marta Wnuczko, Marcelo Santos, Peter Coppin, & Karan Singh. 2011. "Dots, Line, Contour & Surface Edge Trigger Centre-surround Pickup Mechanism." In Eric P. Charles & L. James

Smart, eds., *Studies in Perception & Action: Sixteenth International Conference on Perception and Action*. New York: Psychology Press.

With Marta Wnuczko. 2014. "Pointing to azimuths and elevations of targets: Blind and blindfolded-sighted." *Perception* 43: 117–228.

14

Dominic McIver Lopes

Professor of Philosophy at the University of British Columbia

---

1. Why were you initially drawn to the study of images?

According to family lore, my mother kindled my enthusiasm for pictures when I was an infant — she was an art student and she brought me along on sketching expeditions to the art gallery. Later, I would sneak off after school to the Royal Ontario Museum in Toronto, where I was enthralled by the Egyptian rooms, more for the tomb paintings, sculptures, and hieroglyphics than the mummies. These childish enthusiasms took an intellectual turn when Jim McGilvray at McGill University introduced me to E. H. Gombrich's *Art and Illusion* and Nelson Goodman's *Languages of Art*. Gombrich spoke of images as "equivalences which enable us to see reality in terms of an image and an image in terms of reality" (1960: 345) but Goodman took as his motto Virginia Woolf's wisecrack that an image is not a duplicate of the real world... "one of the damn things is enough" (1976: 3). The differences between what we see when we look at a picture and what we can see with the naked eye struck me as far more interesting than their similarities, but I came to realize that differences matter only against a background of similarities. I felt that powerful images mobilize a fine interplay between their differences from and their similarity to ordinary perception. That turned out to be a fruitful idea and refining it came to occupy me for several years.

2. What do you consider your contribution to the field?

My work on images unfolded in two stages. The one led naturally to the other, though I can't say that was part of a plan.

The first stage culminated in my 1996 book, *Understanding Pictures*, which is really an heir to the work of Gombrich and Goodman. They had asked, how do pictures represent? What is involved in extracting the meaning from a picture? In a kind of caricature, obliterating the great subtlety of the writings of Gombrich and Goodman, some scholars in the 1970s and 80s framed answers to these questions in terms of a simple dichotomy. Either images represent perceptually and we understand them by using ordinary perceptual skills, or images are language-like, they represent by convention, and we understand them because we learn the conventions. The aim of *Understanding Pictures* was to explain how images take advantage of the workings of perception and yet have a language-like character. The idea was that understanding a picture takes advantage of some of the same perceptual mechanisms as we use in ordinary perception, but that these are extended in new ways that may have to be learned and then transmitted culturally. This suggests that we cannot assume that different styles or systems of imaging are equally useful alternatives to each other: some might be better for serving some purposes than others. As I put it in the book, images are perceptual prostheses — like many tools, they enhance our capabilities by building on those very capabilities. They enhance our powers of perception and hence our powers of perceptually-mediated thought.

Having concluded *Understanding Pictures* on that note, I recognized that I should write a sequel about the value of images. A few other philosophers, notably Richard Wollheim, had written about the aesthetic or artistic value of painting and drawing, but nobody had ventured a systematically study of the cognitive value of images — their value as sources of knowledge and insight about the world and its human inhabitants — and nobody had tried to work out the relationship between the cognitive and aesthetic values of images.

On the contrary, any attempt to talk about the value of images had come to be viewed with considerable suspicion in some quarters of the humanities. The dominant line has been that images are to be understood exclusively as instruments in struggles over class, gender, or race. Talk of their perceptually-mediated value has been considered a sneaky way of hiding their ideological function. However, this doctrine raises and does not completely suppress value theory. It prompts the question why images are so effective in ideological struggles, if not for their ties to perception.

Sight and Sensibility (2005) sets out a framework for understanding the value of images as distinctively visual. The framework is modest in the sense that it does not incur metaphysical commitments and does not rest on culturally or historically parochial assumptions. It is also modest in the sense that it describes the perceptual character of images in a very abstract and flexible way. That leaves room for more specific descriptions that key into the specific imaging practices and the purposes they serve in specific historical and cultural contexts. Yet the framework is robust enough to be useful in serious critiques of images — the book concludes with a case study of feminist critiques of the male gaze, showing that they are more forceful when placed in the framework I proposed than when allied to the "hermeneutics of suspicion."

A few of my papers apply these ideas in more specific ways and they illustrate how much work remains to be done in the philosophy of images. "Art Media and the Sense Modalities: Tactile Pictures" (1997) was inspired by the marvelous research by John Kennedy at the University of Toronto on tactile pictures made and used by blind people (Kennedy 1993). This research convinced me that we should think of depiction as a perceptual medium and not necessarily a visual one. "Drawing in a Social Science: Lithic Illustration" (2009) asks the question why a scientist would ever use a drawing instead of a photograph, if her concern is to produce objective data. "An Empathic Eye" (2011) considers how the visuality of images can be harnessed to enhance empathy — it contributes to a renewed appreciation among philosophers and psychologists of the importance of the capacity for empathy. Although empathy is usually understood as engaged by situations grasped through narratives, it can also be engaged by pictorially mediated perception.

Each of these papers links how images represent and are understood, on one hand, to the many different kinds of value they realize on the other hand. Two recent papers, "Nobody Needs a Theory of Art" (2008) and "The Myth of (Non-aesthetic) Artistic Value" (2011) form the core of my most recent book (2014). Here I try to show that it is not a good idea to think of art images as images that share something in common with works of musical art, literary art, and the like. Rather, art images are just the products of one special image-making practice — one that can only be understood in terms of the specific features of images. There is no science of art — only various sciences of the various arts. So when it comes to art images, their being images must always remain in sight.

3. What is the proper role of the study of images in relation to other academic disciplines?

No single discipline enjoys a monopoly on images; they are studied in so many different disciplines — art history, of course, but also philosophy, psychology, anthropology, sociology, communication studies, information science, and computer science, to name a few. This arrangement makes perfect sense to me. Depiction stands alongside language as a fundamental medium of human expression and thought. So while art history has a lot to teach about images, especially those that we have come to consider works of art, delegating the study of images to art history alone would be like assuming that all language is poetry. Likewise, although information science is an increasingly important branch of image studies, there is a great deal more to imaging than carrying information. Like language, images reflect and help to create and sustain social structures, they help us to generate our own conception of ourselves, our histories, and our cultures. To complicate matters, understanding how images accomplish this task is itself part of that very task. We need the expertise of humanists and social scientists to disentangle this knot. So I view the fragmentation of image studies across many disciplines as a strength. Of course, it is also a weakness, simply because it is such a challenge for scholars working on images to share their ideas and their findings when they come from different perspectives, use different vocabularies, and have different goals. For the most part that challenge still lies before us.

4. What do you consider the most important topics and/or contributions in the study of images? and 5. What are the most important open problems in this field and what are the prospects/ avenues for progress?

Some mysteries are obviously mysteries and others are easy to miss. The fact that we can know a language is astonishing to anyone who has watched a child acquire language or who has struggled to communicate with an allophone, but the fact that we can make and interpret images with such ease flies below the radar of our curiosity. Presumably our facility with images lulls us into taking them for granted. A Gombrich or a Goodman is needed to awaken the mystery. At any rate, the serious, comprehensive, and systematic study of images is a remarkably new enterprise. Apart from manuals written for painters, there is little art history until the nineteenth century. Goodman was the first philosopher to take images seriously — as seriously as language. Work on the effective use of images for visualizing information is also relatively new — Otto Neurath's rules of Isotypes are an early example, dating from the 1930s. Any young field offers huge opportunities for new work and hence for making progress. The following wish list is skewed, of course, by the trajectory of my own research.

Image-makers have at their disposal several different representational media and systems of representation. Many of these have been described by Margaret Hagen in *Varieties of Realism: Geometries of Representational Art* (1986) and John Willats in *Art and Representation: New Principles in the Analysis of Pictures* (1997). The next step is to gain a better understanding of the advantages and disadvantages of different representational techniques. Michael Baxandall's superb book, *Patterns of Intention: On the Historical Explanation of Pictures* (1987), supplies a methodology for historical studies along these lines — he advises historians to focus attention on artistic choices as solutions to problems. Edward Tufte's beautiful work brings out the continuity between images and diagrams for data visualization, dramatizes the importance of good imaging for quality reasoning and decision-making, and illustrates what can be achieved through astute case studies. His findings have yet to be grounded in facts about the psychology of picture perception.

Not only do they store information about the world, images also provide instructions. They can be used in declarative or imperative modes. The more complex the technology furnishing our environments, the more taxing the cognitive demands it makes on its users. Images can harness the processing power of the visual and motor centers of the brain to alleviate these demands. However, images designed to direct pragmatic actions are mostly made on a hit-and-miss basis. A science of "command images" is needed.

Images may function on their own or in concert with representations in other media. Moving images have been studied in relation to music and linguistic storytelling. Other kinds of interaction between media are relatively less well studied. The medium of the comic strip is comparably unexplored territory, so is the juxtaposition of images with text (and diagrams and tables of data) in scientific contexts.

The specialization of image-making, which is now concentrated in a tiny population of artists and designers, has been accompanied by an attenuation of drawing education in the schools. Few adults now draw. Can technology provide an answer? After all, although few adults now draw, most make extremely good images with digital cameras, and the world is awash in images as never before — they are added to web sites like flickr at a rate of billions per month. Still, photographs are not drawings and drawings can be used to sketch ideas, to simplify complex scenarios, to outline hypotheses and solutions to problems. A better appreciation of the cognitive value of drawing paired with a more thorough understanding of the psychological mechanisms that underlie drawing might help engineer some applications that will do for the doodle what the CCD did for the portrait.

None of these suggestions requires the special expertise of philosophers. There are plenty of problems remaining in the philosophy of images but it is my bet that the time is now ripe for an intensification of dialogue among scholars of images from different disciplines.

Bibliography

Baxandall, Michael. 1987. *Patterns of Intention: On the Historical Explanation of Pictures*. New Haven: Yale University Press.

Gombrich, Ernst H. 1960. *Art and Illusion*. London: Phaidon.

Goodman, Nelson. 1976. *Languages of Art*. Indianapolis: Hackett.

Hagen, Margaret. 1986. *Varieties of Realism: Geometries of Representational Art*. Cambridge: Cambirdge University Press.

Kennedy, John M. 1993. *Drawing and the Blind: Pictures to Touch.* New Haven: Yale University Press.

Tufte, Edward. 2001. *The Visual Display of Quantitative Information.* Cheshire: Graphics Press.

Willats, John. 1997. *Art and Representation: New Principles in the Analysis of Pictures.* Princeton: Princeton University Press.

Selected publications by Dominic McIver Lopes

1996. *Understanding Pictures.* Oxford: Oxford University Press.

1997. "Art Media and the Sense Modalities: Tactile Pictures." *Philosophical Quarterly* 47: 425–440.

2003a. "Pictures and the Representational Mind." *Monist* 86: 32–52.

2003b. "The Aesthetics of Photographic Transparency." *Mind* 112: 433–448.

2005. *Sight and Sensibility: Evaluating Pictures.* Oxford: Oxford University Press.

2008. "Nobody Needs a Theory of Art." *Journal of Philosophy* 105: 109–127.

2009a. *A Philosophy of Computer Art.* London: Routledge.

2009b. "Drawing in a Social Science: Lithic Illustration." *Perspectives on Science* 17: 5–25.

2011a. "An Empathic Eye." In Peter Goldie & Amy Coplan, eds., *Empathy: Philosophical and Psychological Perspectives.* Oxford: Oxford University Press.

2011b. "The Myth of (Non-Aesthetic) Artistic Value." *Philosophical Quarterly* 61: 518–536.

2014. *Beyond Art.* Oxford: Oxford University Press.

15

Patrick Maynard

Professor Emeritus of Philosophy at the University of Western Ontario

---

1. Why were you initially drawn to the study of images?

"Drawn to" would be where I began, as a child: in drawing, not thinking about, images. But this doesn't get one far in schooling, which must be based on linguistic and mathematical thinking. Coming from a linguistically fluent family — both parents prolific authors — writing seemed natural, so I could rely a lot on that through a formative liberal arts University of Chicago education followed by graduate study. Philosophy only providing slight environment for work in or on visual image-making, formal "study of images" began for me when, for a thesis topic, my Cornell advisor, Frank Sibley, suggested that E. H. Gombrich's recent *Art and Illusion* could use philosophical scrutiny.

Teaching philosophy does allow study of images under one recognized, if marginal, course rubric, that of "aesthetics," though my work never depended on that and I never identified myself that way. In retrospect, I recognize a gradual emergence of our present topic: not so much due to art as such as much as it was to a way of thinking: 'visualizing,' or maybe 'spatializing.' Perhaps one tends to organize texts and ideas spatially, annotate pictorially or at least graphically; one tends to use lots of slides and blackboards — as much for diagrams as words; one tends to at meetings want graphs besides columns of numbers (please, something beyond histograms and pie-charts) especially if imaginative — even witty — and good to look at. Thus a visual design motive uncommon in the field. Well, we think in different ways, different fields and traditions are selective of these, so philosophy filters for other things. Even so, teaching philosophy being not so much a matter of imparting information as of helping people understand things — notably unfamiliar ways of thinking — it entails lots of explaining and thus finding models, analogies, applications, and graphics can be very useful.

Regularly teaching from great philosophers, so getting free of interpretive clichés, one may also discover graphic resources in some of them. Plato, obviously, in his original demonstration in *Menon* and in his use of not just myths and allegories but brilliant visualizations by this arch critic of visual thinking. Thus, *Republic* defends itself as a "diagram," which it mentions erasing and drawing over on a ground, and its Cave of Shadows allegory — completing an original set of visualizations, in which light as shining from a source first breaks into our mental imagery — is introduced with a verb for "see." Galilei's graphics provide another sort of case: indeed, this way of thinking may be more characteristic of scientific philosophers than of those who write about art. Nonetheless, contemporary philosophers tend to consider thought to be propositional and consider language, be it natural or formal, to be its proper vehicle. This is understandable, since that's how truth or acceptability — and thereby logical relationships — can be introduced. Yet, as the histories of philosophy and science show, content is central: thus all the efforts at inventing, promoting, criticizing kinds of conceptions, not just arguments, as philosophers tend to say. That's why it was an encouraging feature of Goodman's (1968) theory that, aside from truth and logical relations, it had graphic and other representations cognitively shaping experience. However, this was a version of 'sign' or 'reference' construals of representations with arrows pointing at things, which I could never understand, in what always struck me as itself a crude and misleading mental graphic, a blackboard cartoon of wide appeal.

2. What do you consider your contribution to the field?

My main efforts so far would be in producing the first full philosophy books on two important topics, photography and drawing, in their many aspects: *The Engine of Visualization: Thinking Through Photography* (Maynard 2000) and *Drawing Distinctions: The Varieties of Graphic Expression* (Maynard 2005). Motivation for both was from the interests indicated; neither could have developed from any 'problem situation' in philosophy since none existed — there being little philosophical literature on either. So, both were solo efforts and took time; both are designed for broader appeal, notably among artists and writers on art — which turned out to be just as well! Also, neither comes out of aesthetics or even focuses on art until their last chapters. The uses and importance of drawing and of photography are far wider than those of any of their arts; besides, we're unlikely to understand them in art without first understanding those matters.

The photo research was done in a series of papers in Gombrich's mode of investigating the functions of images. It seemed obvious that photographs, like other visual images, have always had several easily identifiable main functions, that these can be combined in different ways, and that failure to observe these simple facts lies behind our culture's ongoing mystification regarding them. Reading the various fine histories of photography then available, two more points became clear: first, that, given its continuously changing nature, the topic had to be photography itself rather than the standard reification, "*the* [which?] photograph;" second, that photography has from its outset been not one technology, but a whole family of them — basically, for marking surfaces with light and similar radiations — for doing a variety of things, related to and interacting with other contemporary technologies at more or less distance. This meant thinking about technology generally, and Clifford Hooker's idea that technologies are amplifiers of our powers to do things was all I needed to recast the topic of functions and begin an empirical — basically historical — investigation of what these powers are, thus grounding the philosophical job of "thinking through" the main issues that have puzzled people. The resulting book has a simple thesis, argued in a factually supported yet analytic and (I hope) systematic philosophy of photography, in terms of which its variety of image productions can be understood. Yet writers persist in approaching things, 'photographs,' with a paucity of conceptions, in terms of how they might differ from other things, notably 'hand-made' depictions, rather than in terms of what photography is. No wonder photographers have little use for theorists. Who likes to be described in terms of how someone fancies they differ from someone else — including near relatives?

To be philosophical — to attempt breadth and depth — a book on the ancient, more important, topic of *drawing* needed to extend more broadly to consolidate research on the natures of visual representation itself, perspective, and other matters of debate. With much 'theory' of painting around (in works that hardly mention paint, or even color), high time for a systematic appreciation of drawing, across its many forms and uses, not just art — that is, of "all kinds of drawings." For this, the drawing book attempts to assemble and order a 'tool kit' of conceptions from a number of sources: engineering and design drawing, art criticism and history, cognitive and developmental studies, and so forth — again to provide some richness of conceptions along with real-world, historical context, to suggest why it matters to people. And again, it's a mistake to begin from fine art, although we get there. The modern world, it first argues, is the *drawn* one, demarcated from preceding handcraft millennia by drafting lines: a world of mass-manufactured, complex artifacts that must be drawn many times to be produced, distributed, used. Poor planning nowadays usually implies poor drawing, and we live and work in a lot of that. (Any who consider this mere 'aesthetics' might consider the effects of one incompetent 'butterfly-ballot' design-drawing.)

I hope that both books make cases for nonlinguistic intelligence and creativity. After all, when paleoarcheologists date the emergence of our modern mind and therefore species, what they usually look to is the literally hard evidence of the first images, not language, which is only (rather swiftly) inferred from it. I also hope my subsequent writings defend images against a more recent trend to reduce image content, if not now to language, then to the environmentally visual, through fashionable 'it's just seeing' approaches of the cognitive — increasingly, neuro — sciences, which tend to forget that we not only have brains but use them, like other organs of our bodies. In all this, autonomy of images remains the focus.

4. What do you consider the most important topics and/or contributions in the study of images?

If we may defer answer to Question 3, my list of main contributors begins with Gombrich, who risked venturing into the field of perception studies to revolutionize our understanding of convincingness in visual images. That was mainly in *Art and Illlusion*, a still poorly understood book. It's so lucid, rich, open in discussion and examples that aspects can be appreciated by those with slight grasp of the whole. Like most historians of Western art, Gombrich had relied on some standard conceptions, including that of naturalism in depiction, but his unusually reflective mind wondered why naturalism has histories, including significant reversals. Having, with his 'function of the image' idea, already freed himself from prevailing holistic 'spirit' of the age (including modern) or culture approaches, he drew on the latest perception science critically to understand how effective depiction works — thus going beyond naturalism into caricature (where he actually began), expressiveness, and so forth. He worked a revolution, dispelling the old, mesmerizing idea of 'the imitation of appearances' by refuting the idea of things called "appearances" that could be imitated. Nevertheless, this idea continues to appeal, even at theoretical levels, impeding understanding of images.

I think that Gombrich's breakthrough may be simply described. He took from contemporary vision research its discovery of the modularity of perception, based on controlled experiments separating and testing varieties of discrete cues, such as occlusion, highlight, shadow and gradients of size, texture and so forth. Regarding images, he was the first to explain how compelling representation consists in discovering such cues and testing their efficacies by trial and error, given a remarkable characteristic of vision, that recognition can work off an extremely limited biological cue repertoire, which practicing image-makers had been probing long before there was science to study it. In this he made critical use of Gestalt ideas and also drew on Niko Tinbergen's and Konrad Lorenz's work on supernormal stimuli. In short, 'looking like' is 'like-looking:' images can 'look like' things when looking at images is like looking at things — that is, exploits similar mechanisms. Gombrich noted that such effects will be more or less peculiar to our visual systems — different creatures would need different cue combinations — and, like all perceptual phenomena, are of course strongly affected by context and framing. But, contrary to much recent neuroscience, Gombrich's approach was strongly contextual, so never reductivist, even regarding what are now called "bottom-up" features. Thus he could provide ample scope for cultural historians to explain how, from a natural basis that withstands relativism, there arises endless creative variation. We use and do things to our brains for our various purposes.

To explain what naturalism is and how it works, Gombrich didn't have to say what depiction is. That was left to Kendall Walton's (1990) *Mimesis as Make-Believe*'s systematic theory, placing it in a broader context of representation, fiction, make-believe, and imagining. Depiction being a kind of representation, we need to understand the latter in order to understand it: thus, while fools still rush in with hopeless picture 'theories' (usually versions of 'imitation of appearances') of representations, *Mimesis* shrewdly delays the topic until two-thirds the way along. One of the important philosophical achievements of its time, the book should be known in fields beyond philosophy — for, while subtitled 'arts,' its approach has important applications for many kinds of activity including, besides developmental and cognitive psychology, any that deal with diagrams, maps, and related representations.

I regret I can't say something similar of Richard Wollheim's (1987) image theory. However his central topic was ever, as he stated late, "painting, which has this great tradition in Europe [that] really gets going to my mind at a certain date, something like 1520." So the three-hundred images in his *Painting as an Art* exclude fresco, Giotto and Masaccio, barely mention Leonardo, Michelangelo, Raphael, or tempera (Duccio, Piero). Absent watercolor, medievals and a millennium of Asian art miss the cut. Thus a sensibility for Venetian oil painting, critically articulated as for "a sense of the actual way that the brush deposited material on the surface" (Wollheim 2003). Splendid, but not an inductive basis for a theory of visual depiction, even as a fine art, certainly not for a philosophy of visual representation.

Yet its influence lingers, opposite to Gombrich's and Walton's openings of "the field of image studies," ironically at a time of great expansion in popular access to the varied cultural riches that fast-growing museums, reproduction technologies, and websites make accessible.

Still, Wollheim's other contributions are significant, and I'd like to add two original researchers who studied with him: Michael Podro (1998) — who, besides bringing philosophy into art-historical studies, stands out for his subtle defense of depiction as fully visual, yet a stuff of thought, against fashionable treatment of pictures as externalities, visual targets, falling under general visual theory — and John Willats (1997, 2005), from whose combination of engineering training and artistic craft, he produced not only original contributions to psychology of child drawing but lucid clarification of a perpetual cultural mystifier, perspective, among other drawing systems. For the technological expansion noted, our 'genius' might be Edward Tufte, in a series of original works on the principles of good visual presentation of quantitative information, causal explanation, and so forth. This might introduce Question 5 — after a brief response to 3.

3. What is the proper role of the study of images in relation to other academic disciplines?

Thus the inspiring company of a few working in relative isolation. But with "academic disciplines," we get to joint research and difficult topics like curriculum. I wouldn't wish to see undergraduate "communication," "information/media," or "visual culture" university programs eroding precious arts and sciences education. But, regarding existing arts and sciences subjects, it may be time to go back over the history of thought in terms of use of images, not as limited to fine art: indeed one would like to see it featured in earlier school subjects. Perhaps more likely might be technical institutes, where we can already assume sufficient background of graphical awareness as basis for historical and theoretical work. Postgraduate studies and institutes seem to me promising, and it's heartening to see the emergence of supported research groups. Of course, within universities, the push is coming anyway out of background culture, as digitalization entails increasing visualization for successive generations of students, permeating all subjects. This leads to Question 5, regarding "open problems" and "prospects/avenues," which nowadays include infographing, knowledge mapping, data visualizing, and so forth.

5. What are the most important open problems in this field and what are the prospects/avenues for progress?

I suggest two things. First, with rapidly advancing technologies — notably, digital — together with the growth of marketing, we find ourselves faced willy-nilly with large image topics. As computation technologies vastly increase data collection, storage, structuring, and retrieval, they overwhelm our linguistic and mathematical resources for accessing and interpreting data. Several sciences seem now in a sort of Baconian age, where detection via data sensing and analysis are frequently in the news. Thus visualization's triumph: for digitalization allows us to shape its data to our great natural sense-processing powers for finding patterns, comprehending, discovering, and communicating. Particular aspects of our biological sight, sound, touch, and movement systems are increasingly mobilized to deal with burgeoning data sets. Millions of years of evolution being given to visual processing, no wonder we seek interfaces with the visual cortex — although, as touch screens lately show, not exclusively. So, digitalization's power of translation comes to the rescue, as even the interactive graphics of today's online newspapers delight and inform. Of course, besides quantitative representation, other kinds of visual imaging, notably from astronomy and medicine, are prominent.

In a cited remark, Alexander von Humboldt wrote that "statistical projections which speak to the senses without fatiguing the mind, possess the advantage of fixing the attention on a great number of important facts" (1811: cxxxiii). Tufte adds the important point that graphic presentation is an ethical act, something done for others, to put them in better position for action: to judge relevantly and fairly for themselves. Yet, as Plato argued and visual illusionists delight to remind us, our senses are whimsically shaped, with startling gaps and defects not flagged by their systems, and hence prey to magicians and less benign sophists. Modern cognitive psychology maps these vagaries — yet, with modern marketing, far more resources are devoted to exploiting than to understanding with them. As leading adman George Lois stated, ads are "poison gas" capable of "manufacturing any feeling you want" (Prey 2009). Regarding the topics just outlined, "know thyself" calls for sustained — well-supported — seriously-informed technical and historical research: that is, not too specialized, but critical and always within broader contexts of understanding, including the riches of the past. Given increasingly easy access to the world's legacy of images, we should be better able to understand, appreciate, and learn from many societies, through time around the world.

Second, for philosophy and related cognitive studies, I think the main challenge remains in placing images within an adequate, broader account of mental 'representations,' which centrally includes language while not being so limited by it. Here, despite current interest in the nature of consciousness, logocentric obstacles remain formidable. For example, some current paleoanthropological theory running contrary to what I stated before, it's not surprising when a scientist treats the place of image-making in our evolution in terms of "decorative art" or "symbolism" generally, even as weak evidence for the advent of language as the defining event while considering stenciled handprints more exciting

(Dunbar 2014: 261, 235, 290). Thus, theorists who would be thrilled by evidence of a Lower Paleolithic linguistic utterance, say, with the content, "lioness refusing male lion's show of interest," despite its not being propositional, pass over the fact that we were meant to recognize marks in Chauvet Cave as placed by skilled, practiced hands, in order to bring us vividly to imagine seeing this and much more — thereby satisfying the five levels of intentionality or mentalising required to define the modern human mind (Dunbar 2014: 242). Yet the difference we usually emphasize between that mind and the earlier, including its nearest kin species, is, beyond intelligent response to immediate environments, the ability deliberately to put mental productions before ourselves and others, as embodied imaginings — even as images — for consideration. It is that which, over thirty-thousand years later, has made us a miracle and menace on this planet.

Finally, the above attention to data visualization is not meant to detract from detailed study of art. For me, besides being visual — probably, synaesthetic — the main issue in common for all these studies is freedom of the mind, and there art always leads the way.

Bibliography

Dunbar, Robin. 2014. *Human Evolution*. London: Penguin.

Gombrich, Ernst. 1960. *Art and Illusion: A Study in the Psychology of Pictorial Representation*. New York: Pantheon.

Goodman, Nelson. 1968. *Languages of Art: An Approach to a Theory of Symbols*. Indianapolis: Bobbs-Merrill.

von Humboldt, Alexander. 1811. *Political Essay on the Kingdom of New Spain*, vol. 1. New York: AMS Press.

Podro, Michael. 1998. *Depiction*. New Haven: Yale University Press.

Pray, Doug, dir. *Art & Copy*. 2009.

Tufte, Edward. 1990. *Envisioning Information*. Cheshire: Graphics Press.

Walton, Kendall. 1990. *Mimesis as Make-Believe: On the Foundations of Representational Arts*. Cambridge: Harvard University Press.

Willats, John. 1997. *Art and Representation: New Principles in the Analysis of Pictures*. Princeton: Princeton University Press.

Willats, John. 2005. *Making Sense of Children's Drawings*. Mahwah: Lawrence Erlbaum.

Wollheim, Richard. 1987. *Painting as an Art*. Princeton: Princeton University Press.

Wollheim, Richard. 2003. Interview by John Rapko. San Francisco Art Institute. https://www.academia.edu/4829390/Richard_Wollheim_interviewed_by. Accessed 14 January 2015.

Selected publications by Patrick Maynard

1997. *The Engine of Visualization: Thinking Through Photography.* Ithaca: Cornell University Press.

2005. *Drawing Distinctions: The Varieties of Graphic Expression.* Ithaca: Cornell University Press.

2009. "Review of Cretien van Campen, The Hidden Sense: Synesthesia in Art and Science." *Art Bulletin* 91, 3: 385–388.

2011. "What Drawing Draws On: The Relevance of Current Vision Research." *Rivista di Estetica: Disegno* 47, 2: 9–29.

2012a. "Arts, Agents, Artifacts: Photography's Automatisms." *Critical Inquiry: Agency and Automatism: Photography and Art Since the Sixties* 38, 4: 727–745.

2012b. "What's So Funny? Comic Content in Depiction." In Aaron Meskin & Roy T. Cook, eds., *The Art of Comics: A Philosophical Approach*, 105–124. Malden: Wiley-Blackwell.

Forthcoming. "Wayfinding: Notes on the 'Public' as Interactive." *Review of Philosophy and Psychology: Pictorial and Spatial Representation.*

16
W. J. T. Mitchell

Gaylord Donnelley Distinguished Service Professor of English and Art History at the University of Chicago

---

1. Why were you initially drawn to the study of images?
The attraction came from several directions simultaneously. First, my Roman Catholic upbringing gave me a sense of the metaphysical importance of images, and the need to discriminate critically between an over- and underestimation of their power. I learned very early the distinctions between idolatry (adoration) and veneration (love) of images, and hence both their potential danger and their wonderful capacity for producing feeling and understanding. Second, my training in mathematics, especially geometry, led me to wonder at the marvelous gap and the possible translatability of sequential, algebraic signs and graphic, spatial diagrams; you might call this the mathematical version of the word and image problem. Third, I have an innate tendency to visualize abstractions, to turn verbal descriptions into concretely imagined scenes, and to transform verbal metaphors into mental pictures. Fourth, when I see an image, I seem to go inside it, to look around at the world it opens up, and then to look back at my own world from the image's point of view.

2. What do you consider your contribution to the field?
I have tried to address images on their own terms, not by imposing a theory on them drawn from semiotics, art history, psychology, or philosophy. My aim has been to "picture theory," as my book by that title suggests. I think of myself as a hunter-gatherer of images, following their trail where it leads across the whole range of media, from literature to the visual arts, from poetry to painting to photography to sculpture to cinema to architecture. I have been especially drawn to what I call "metapictures," images that reflect on the nature of images, showing how they are produced, how they affect us, what we do to and with them.

3. What is the proper role of the study of images in relation to other academic disciplines?

I have suggested that we need to revive the ancient discipline of iconology, the study of images across the media. This is a discipline that would intersect with aesthetics, art history, media studies, visual culture, poetics, and rhetoric, but it would not be reducible to any of these disciplines. It would undertake to investigate the ontology of images in social and historical contexts, the "being" of images, not as invariable essences, but their "being in the world." It would also take up the question of the image, not merely as a representation of something, but as the form, frame, or structure through which perception and cognition take place – both the "thing," and the screen or template through which the thing is seen and represented.

4. What do you consider the most important topics and/or contributions in the study of images?

The central topics in the study of images are meaning (hermeneutics), power (rhetoric), and vitality or desire (poetics and erotics). Obviously images are central to the study of the arts, but I think we should not confine them to the sphere of aesthetics, but consider their function in mathematics, sciences, and technology, their role in religion as objects of worship or abomination, and their place in everyday life as constitutive elements of consciousness in both the human and the animal.

5. What are the most important open problems in this field and what are the prospects/avenues for progress?

There are many open problems. It is only a question of the imagination (obviously a key faculty for this field!) to determine what they are. I think the questions of vitalism and animism have emerged in recent years as topics of keen interest, and they have predictably aroused anxiety and resistance, since (as everyone knows) images are not "really" alive. They only seem to be alive under certain conditions. But this "seeming" is worthy of study, of theoretical and historical reflection. That is what I tried to open up to investigation in *What Do Pictures Want?* (Mitchell 2004). These questions of the "life of images" lead us off in two apparently opposite directions: one is anthropological and psychological – toward questions of religion and superstition, magical thinking, delusions and hallucinations, dreams, fantasies, memories, and practices of piety; the other is toward science, especially the life sciences. Contemporary biologists such as Norman MacLeod have argued that life itself (as opposed to the individual living thing) has to be located in the images that link the evolutionary and genetic sequence of organisms. More generally, it seems increasingly obvious that the scientific object, the thing that scientists study, is never a concrete, singular specimen, but an image – i.e., a model, schematic representation, or prototype. Images, in other words, are to pictures as species are to specimens. Are these remarks merely analogical speculations? Or the opening for further research? I think analogy is itself a form of imagery – of Peircean iconicity – and thus an opening on a prospect for progressive thought. Where that thought will lead us remains to be seen.

17

Bence Nanay

Professor of Philosophy and BOF Research Professor at the University of Antwerp and Senior Research Associate at Peterhouse, University of Cambridge

---

1. Why were you initially drawn to the study of images?

I grew up in Budapest, Hungary, where, at least back in the early nineties, there were more than one hundred operating movie theatres, many of which were independent cinemas showing old subtitled black and white films. As a 14–15 year old, I mainly watched mainstream Hollywood films with my friends, but this all changed when at age 16 — for very non-aesthetics reasons — I happened to sit through a retrospective of Michelangelo Antonioni's early films.

What really shocked me — and shocked is the right word — is how each and every one of the images was perfect — one amazing composition after another for two hours (besides the themes of alienation that are bound to be fascinating for a 16 year old). So, I went on to watch all the Antonioni films several times — again, it was easy to do so on big screen at that time in Budapest. And then on to the other grand Italian and French directors of the 1960s, and then on to the silent classics of the 1920s, and so on. So the question really began to bug me: what is it about images that makes some of them beautiful and some others perfectly ordinary? What is it that Antonioni's compositions have but the framing of, say, *Pretty Woman* doesn't?

I wound up working as a film critic for much of my 20s — but this, again, worked out differently in Hungary with its very strong presence of cultural quarterlies, monthlies and weeklies, where it was possible to work as a professional film critic without doing any weekly (i.e., Hollywood) film reviews. I could write about my favorite auteurs, Godard, Resnais, Antonioni, Pasolini, Buñuel, Straub-Huillet, Kiarostami, Tarkovsky, Jarman, and, to go closer to the present, Wong Kar Wai, Raúl Ruiz, Tsai Ming-liang, Jia Zhang Ke, Lisandro Alonso, or Apichatpong Weerasethakul — and get paid for it. It was not a bad life.

But I became increasingly frustrated by the fact that I still didn't really understand what makes beautiful images beautiful. So while working as a film critic, I also continued studying philosophy and aesthetics, graduating with a triple degree of philosophy/aesthetics/film studies. I went on to the philosophy PhD program at the University of California, Berkeley — mainly in order to study with Richard Wollheim.

During graduate school, I was trying to juggle academia and film criticism, as I became a member of FIPRESCI, the International Association of Film Critics, and spent a significant amount of my grad student time at film festivals. One good thing about FIPRESCI is that it sends jury members to various film festivals — I served on the jury at the San Francisco International Film Festival, the Chicago International Film Festival, the Miami International Film Festival, the Mar del Plata International Film Festival, the Pula International Film Festival, etc. And life on the 'festival circuit,' as it is called, is very different from and much more glamorous than the grad student life of sitting in the library and going to seminars.

One important thing I learned during this time on the 'festival circuit' is how radically critics differ in their assessment of the artistic merits and demerits of films. This really becomes more than a theoretical issue during those long and heated discussions about which films should get the award. Some critics — many working at very prestigious journals/magazines — seemed to have diametrically opposed taste from mine. But it was also reassuring, and philosophically interesting, to see that some other critics had the almost exact same preference for films as I did — in spite of cultural and age differences.

In spite of the glamour of the world of international film criticism, I decided to focus on philosophy, mainly because given the everyday politics and pragmatics of film criticism, the burning question that made me choose this path to begin with — namely, the one about what makes good images good — had taken the back seat and I was itching to get back to try to answer this question. In the meantime, Richard Wollheim, who had became a really close friend, besides being my supervisor, died and I changed dissertation topics to focus on philosophical issues concerning the human mind — with an eye to understanding how the mind works when we are looking at pictures and especially at good pictures.

2. What do you consider your contribution to the field?

I firmly believe that if we want to understand images, we need to understand how we see them. I have argued that all the interesting questions about images are, at the end of the day, questions about our perception (Nanay 2013, 2014). Thus, if we want to understand what makes pictures pictures, we need to consider how we perceive pictures (this is a thought I inherited from Richard Wollheim). And, importantly, in order to understand what makes good images good images, we also need to examine how our perceptual system functions.

I want to talk about four questions that I have been trying to answer. They are intertwined in various interesting ways. (i) What happens in our mind when we perceive pictures: how is it different to see a drawing or a photograph of an apple and to see the apple face to face?(ii) Why do we like looking at pictures? Is there something about picture perception that is in itself somehow enjoyable or gives rise to an aesthetic experience? (iii) Can we make sense of the claim that it is the formal features of a picture that play a crucial role in explaining why we like some pictures and dislike others (and do so without falling prey to the objections to classic formalism)? (iv) How can we explain that we like some pictures and dislike others? Is this a difference between the intrinsic values of the pictures themselves or a difference between our own experiences?

(i) What is the difference between seeing a drawing or a photograph of an apple and seeing it face to face? Is there something that makes picture perception special? My answer is simple: when we see pictures, our perceptual system works differently from the way it works when we see something face to face (Nanay 2004, 2005, 2008, 2010, 2011, 2014). To put it very simply, we see both the depicted object and the surface of the picture. The crucial issue is to clarify what is meant by 'seeing' in this claim. Seeing here does not mean conscious perception. Perception does not have to be conscious and in fact it is very often unconscious. So in order to see something in a picture, we don't need to consciously attend to both the picture surface and the depicted object — this can happen, but not very often. What is needed for picture perception is that we see (consciously or unconsciously) both the surface and the depicted object.

I substantiate these claims with some emphasis on an important fact about the human perceptual system. Neuroscience teaches us that visual processing happens in two more or less independent channels. To put it very simply, the 'dorsal system' helps us to perform actions while the 'ventral system' helps us to identify and recognize objects (Milner & Goodale 1995, Jeannerod 1997). These two subsystems work in unison most of the time, but they can come apart, for example in those patients who have brain damage in either the dorsal or the ventral stream. If they have a functioning dorsal stream but lesions in the ventral stream, they will (I'm simplifying a bit) be able to perform visually guided actions, like posting an envelope, without much trouble. But they will not be able to recognize or identify the objects they are performing these actions with. And conversely, if a patient has lesions in the dorsal stream, but a healthy ventral stream, then she can recognize, identify, and describe her environment, but will have trouble performing even the simplest perceptually guided actions (again, I am simplifying a bit).

In the case of some perceptual illusions, the functioning of these two visual subsystems can come apart even in healthy adult humans. Some perceptual illusions can fool the ventral processing, but not the dorsal one. But in this case, the two subsystems still represent the same object, but they represent them differently (one incorrectly, one more or less correctly).

My proposal is that when we perceive pictures, the dorsal (action-guiding) stream represents the picture surface, whereas the ventral (identification-focused) stream represents the depicted object. There are empirical reasons to think that this is the right way of thinking about picture perception (people with lesions in one of the two visual subsystems have problems – different problems – with picture perception). And this way of thinking about picture perception could also be thought of as an elaboration on my old teacher Richard Wollheim's concept of 'twofoldness,' the idea that picture perception involves twofold perception, one fold directed at the surface, the other at the depicted scene.

(ii) This account of picture perception is supposed to be true of any and all instances of picture perception. Not only of admiring the brushstrokes on a Corot painting in a museum, but also of watching television shows or looking at postcards or family photographs. But picture perception is sometimes more than this. It sometimes leads to the appreciation of pictures as pictures. Sometimes we like looking at pictures not because of what they depict but, to put it simply, because of the way they depict their subject. What happens in these cases?

My proposal here is that in these cases (that I call, following Michael Podro, 'inflected' experiences) we are consciously attending both to the picture surface and to the depicted scene. One way of putting this is that we are attending to the relation between the two: to how the depicted scene emerges from the brushstrokes on the surface (Nanay 2010, 2012a, 2012b, 2014).

Although this may sound similar to my story about picture perception in general, it is a very different claim. It is true of all instances of picture perception that we see (that is, perceptually represent) both the surface and the depicted scene. This does not imply conscious attention to the surface. And, as the perceptual processing in the dorsal steam is normally unconscious, we normally perceive the surface unconsciously. But in those special cases when we appreciate pictures aesthetically, it is not only dorsally and unconsciously that we perceive the picture surface, we also allocate some conscious attention to it. While the claim about picture perception in general was a claim about twofold perceptual representation, the claim I make about the aesthetic appreciation of pictures is about twofold conscious attention.

In other words, the aesthetic appreciation of pictures requires some degree of distributed attention: we need to attend, simultaneously, both to the surface and to the depicted scene (and maybe also to the relation between the two). I think that this distributed attention is a very important feature of aesthetic experiences in general (not just the aesthetic experience of pictures, but also of nature, of everyday objects or of non-pictorial works of art). As the appreciation of pictures as pictures necessarily involves this distributed attention, it may be an important step to understand aesthetic experiences in general (without necessarily leading to the controversial claim that we can only have aesthetic experiences of a natural landscape because we have seen many pictures of landscapes).

(iii) I consider myself to be a formalist in some sense — in a sense that I'm sure many genuine formalists would not call formalist at all. Formalists claim that it is only the formal properties of pictures that are responsible for their aesthetic value. Or, to put it somewhat differently, when we appreciate pictures aesthetically, we are appreciating their formal properties. It is an open question just what these formal properties may be. Some paradigmatic formal properties are colors, shapes, and their combinations — properties of the picture surface, including the picture's composition.

Formalism is remarkably unpopular these days — in academic circles. But academics — philosophers, art historians and cultural theorists — still find it important to argue against it because of its popular appeal. I think we may be able to salvage the gist of formalism in such a way that would retain this popular appeal but avoid the various problems with this view that philosophers and art historians like to emphasize.

My way of doing this is to loosen the concept of formal properties: I take formal properties to be properties that cannot be fully characterized without reference to some of the surface properties of the picture (Nanay 2014). So classic formal properties (like shape and color) would count as formal properties in my sense, but the full set of formal properties in my sense would include much more. Importantly, the relation between the surface properties of the picture and some properties of the depicted scene would also count as formal properties in my sense — something some of the classic formalists, like Clive Bell or Clement Greenberg, would clearly not be too happy with. And even the relation between the surface properties of the picture and the socio-historical context or the author's intention would count as formal properties — classic formalists would be even less happy with this.

Does this broadening of the concept of formal properties make formalism a completely vacuous view that has no opponents? No. Formalism in my sense is incompatible with the views according to which what is valuable about a picture has nothing to do with its surface properties (and these views have a lot of proponents, especially in the tradition of psychoanalytic and Marxist art criticism).

(iv) The last two questions were about the aesthetic appreciation of pictures. My view is that it is a matter of consciously attending to both the surface and the depicted scene — to a formal property in my sense. But one very important question remains open. What makes us enjoy some pictures and not others? Why do we appreciate aesthetically some pictures and not others? Is this a difference between the intrinsic value of the pictures themselves or a difference between our own experiences?

This is really just a different way of asking probably the most basic question of aesthetics: is beauty a real feature of the work of art or is it in the eye of the beholder? The default view among academics and definitely among analytic philosophers is that beauty, or aesthetic value, is real — it is out there waiting for us to discover and enjoy it. The view is called aesthetic realism. In contrast, in all the aesthetics classes I have taught, the vast majority of students did not buy this picture at all. Almost all of them were convinced that beauty was in the eye of the beholder. Of course, this question leads to various grand debates in metaphysics about the nature of aesthetic properties — but the focus on perception in understanding images and the aesthetic value of images may help us, if not to argue for the aesthetic antirealist position (according to which beauty is in the eye of the beholder), then at least to make this view a plausible alternative to aesthetic realism.

The starting point here is the well-known psychological phenomenon called the Mere Exposure Effect. Very simply, it shows that the more we are exposed to a stimulus the more likely we are to evaluate it positively. Most of the research on the Mere Exposure Effect has been on non-aesthetic and non-pictorial domains, but it has been shown that the same is true of the aesthetic evaluation of pictures: the more we see them, the more likely we are to evaluate them positively.

There is a lot of further research that would need to be done on this. Most of the research on the Mere Exposure Effect regarding picture perception was on the aesthetic evaluation of the very same token picture as the one we had been exposed to. But the relevant finding from the point of view of aesthetic antirealism would be if mere exposure to a type of picture, or, even better, to some higher order visual property such as composition, made the positive evaluation of pictures of the same type (or of different instantiations of the same higher order visual property) more likely. Further, our encounters with pictures are very rarely value-free. When we see pictures in a museum or in an art album, there is an implicit assumption that these pictures must be aesthetically valuable (otherwise they wouldn't be there). And we know from the psychological literature that if the exposure is value-laden, then the effect is even stronger than in the case of mere (that is, value-free) exposure.

How does this help the antirealist? It could at least begin to explain how the reason why we like some pictures but not others may have to do with the pictures we have seen earlier in our life (and maybe not with the intrinsic quality of the perceived picture itself). It may also give an antirealist explanation to a phenomenon that has been the trump card in the realists' hands: aesthetic agreements. Very few people would say that Jack Vettriano's paintings are better than Vermeer's. How can we explain this? The realist has a simple answer: Vermeer's pictures are just better. What can the antirealist say? If beauty and aesthetic value is in the eye of the beholder, how can we explain that almost all of these beholders prefer Vermeer to Vettriano?

And here is where the Mere Exposure Effect (or, the value-laden exposure effect) can help. Most people have seen more Vermeer pictures (or pictures that share higher order visual features, such as compositions with Vermeer paintings) in a value-laden context than Vettriano pictures (or pictures that share higher order visual features, such as compositions with Vettriano paintings). Vermeer (and painters whose paintings share higher order visual features, such as compositions with Vermeer's) is part of the canon and we have way more visual access to pictures in the canon than those not. And because of the Mere Exposure Effect, this, and not some opaque reference to intrinsic value, is what explains why we tend to like them.

Is this a depressing view? A little bit. But maybe not that much. According to this view, it is not the intrinsic properties of the painting that make you like it, but your own perceptual history. This shouldn't take away from one's enjoyment — in some ways it could even be argued that according to this view, there is something much more special about this picture for you specifically.

But regardless of whether this view is depressing, if it is correct, it has far-reaching consequences. If aesthetic value is a matter of previous exposure, then we can't take it for granted that in a couple (or a couple of dozens of) generations we will still be surrounded by the pictures (or the kind of pictures) we admire today. If we want our grand-grandkids to look at Vermeers and not Vettrianos (we may or may not want this — I do), we need to make sure that the next generation and the one after that gets exposed to the likes of Vermeer.

Further, if the antirealist story is correct, we really need to be careful what pictures we are looking at. Our taste is determined by what pictures we look at. So in some ways it is dangerous to look at bad pictures! We have no actual defense mechanism against them. Even the mere exposure to them will make us more likely to like them. Be careful what pictures you are looking at!

3. What is the proper role of the study of images in relation to other academic disciplines?

I feel very strongly about the interaction between the study of images and the study of perception and the mind. My approach is based on the assumption that in order to understanding images, we need to understand our mental processes when we are looking at images. This means that the study of images, in my book, needs to rely heavily not only on philosophy of mind and of perception, but also on the empirical sciences of the mind: psychology, cognitive science, vision science, even neuroscience.

I think of this relation between the study of images and the study of the mind as a two-directional one: I have been mainly focusing on the ways in which the study of images depends on the study of the mind, but the converse is also true: many, maybe even most, experiments in vision science involve the perception of various pictures. In order to interpret these experiments properly, we need an account of what picture perception is. I also believe that the study of images has interesting and complex relations to the study of society in general — more about this below.

4. What do you consider the most important topics and/or contributions in the study of images?

I'll take this question to be an invitation to talk about my favorite authors. And I'll start with Heinrich Wölfflin (Wölfflin 1988, 1901, 1915). Wölfflin is not exactly very fashionable these days, but I think he was probably the thinker who knew most about images. Reading Wölfflin invariably makes me happy in a way reading philosophy never does — it's really the second best thing after actually looking at images. While his distinction between painterly and linear style has been criticized *ad nauseam* for not describing the distinction between 16th and 17th Century art appropriately (or fully), the conceptual apparatus he developed could be argued to apply much more widely — an amazing project (and one I am alas not qualified for) would be to trace various aspects of the linear/painterly distinction throughout the history of images. Of all those who wrote about images, Wölfflin did the most for understanding what difference the composition of a picture makes — any attempts at analyzing different kinds of pictorial organization should start with him.

I also have an immense appreciation for Michael Baxandall — I used to go about saying that the best book I have ever read is his *Painting and Experience in Fifteenth Century Italy*. While I would now qualify this claim, this book very clearly demonstrates that an approach that aims to understand images through analyzing the mental processes of perceiving images does not have to be insensitive to various cultural factors — it does not imply biologizing pictures. Baxandall shows how culture can make a huge difference in our perception of pictures and in some ways the analysis of the perception of pictures cannot be accomplished without paying attention to the cultural context.

Finally, it's not only because he was my teacher, but I do think that Richard Wollheim had a huge influence on how we (or, at least we philosophers) think about images. His much criticized concept of twofoldness is probably the most important clue to understanding picture perception (see especially Wollheim 1980, 1987).

5. What are the most important open problems in this field and what are the prospects/avenues for progress?

One topic I have not mentioned but one that is extremely important is the role images play in our society. This is a topic that is rarely touched upon in the analytic philosophy tradition I am working within, but it is one of the most intriguing avenues for research. It has been said that we see more images and see them more often than at any time before in the course of history and it would be important to examine the consequences of this.

A related issue that I am more and more interested in (again, not an analytic philosophy subject, although it has a huge literature within cultural studies) is how images can influence our way of relating to society. More precisely, how do images impact our implicit biases? We know that most people have implicit biases towards (or against) certain racial and gender groups (see the famous Harvard Implicit Association Test that anyone can try out online). The question is: how do we acquire these implicit biases and how can we get rid of them? And images may play a key role in answering both questions. Many of the images we see on a daily (or hourly) basis could be argued to strengthen our implicit bias and if we want to live in a society where people would have no implicit bias, we may have to change the images that get fed to our perceptual system all the time — sitcoms we catch on the plane, films, the images of television commercials, of ads in glossy magazines, of giant posters by the highway, of the pop-up ads on our computers, etc.

A lot would need to be done to make this line of thought more precise; cultural theorists and feminist film theorists (among others) have done a lot already. But maybe the study of images as part of philosophy of perception, the line I am advocating, could be especially helpful. In order to understand how our mind changes to form implicit biases in response to images, we need to analyze the mental processes of picture perception and those further mental processes (of forming or getting rid of implicit biases) that picture perception gives rise to. In some ways this project is more important and crucial than any other (including my own) concerning images. If we want to live in a non-racist, non-sexist society, we need to be surrounded by non-racist, non-sexist images.

Bibliography

Baxandall, Michael. 1972. *Painting and Experience in Fifteenth Century Italy*. Oxford: Oxford University Press.

Jeannerod, Marc. 1997. *The Cognitive Neuroscience of Action*. Oxford: Blackwell.

Milner, A. David & Melvyn A. Goodale. 1995. *The Visual Brain in Action*. Oxford: Oxford University Press.

Wollheim, Richard. 1980. *Art and its Objects*. Cambridge: Cambridge University Press.

Wollheim, Richard. 1987. *Painting as an Art*. Princeton: Princeton University Press.

Wölfflin, Heinrich. 1888. *Renaissance and Baroque*. Ithaca: Cornell University Press.

Wölfflin, Heinrich. 1901/1952. *Classic Art*. London: Phaidon.

Wölfflin, Heinrich. 1915/1932. *Principles of Art History*. New York: Dover Publications.

Selected publications by Bence Nanay

2004. "Taking Twofoldness Seriously. Walton on Imagination and Depiction." *Journal of Aesthetics and Art Criticism* 62: 285–289.

2005. "Is Twofoldness Necessary for Representational Seeing?" *British Journal of Aesthetics* 45: 263–272.

2008. "Picture perception and the two visual subsystems." In Bradley Love, Ken McRae, & Vladimir Sloutsky, eds., *Proceedings of the 30th Annual Conference of the Cognitive Science Society (CogSci 2008)*. Hillsdale: Lawrence Erlbaum, 975–980.

2009. "Narrative pictures." *Journal of Aesthetics and Art Criticism* 67: 119–129.

2010. "Inflected and uninflected perception of pictures." In Catharine Abell & Katarina Bantilaki, eds., *Philosophical Perspectives*

> *on Depiction.* Oxford: Oxford University Press, 181–207.

2011. "Perceiving pictures." *Phenomenology and the Cognitive Sciences* 10: 461–480.

2012a. "The macro and the micro: Andreas Gursky's aesthetics." *Journal of Aesthetics and Art Criticism* 70: 91–100.

2012b. "Anti-pornography: André Kertész's." *Distortions.* In Hans Maes & Jerrold Levinson, eds., *Art and Pornography.* Oxford: Oxford University Press, 191–205.

2013. *Between Perception and Action.* Oxford: Oxford University Press.

2014. *Aesthetics as Philosophy of Perception.* Oxford: Oxford University Press.

18

Barbara Maria Stafford

William B. Ogden Distinguished service Professor Emerita at the University of Chicago

---

1. Five to One

I see my contribution to the field as two-fold: first, to have incorporated the larger world of images into art history and to conceive of that discipline as intrinsically multidisciplinary. My work demonstrates that all sorts of imagery beyond that deriving from drawing, painting, sculpture, and architecture should be part of the imagist's purview. "It is stunning to realize how long the medium — that embattled third space stretching between ourselves and an obscure yonder — has been saturated with [optical] technology" (Stafford 2001: 65). In a Poundian moment, I even proposed that we call ourselves imagists to capture the ambition of understanding images no matter how or where they might lead.

Second, I fought the hydra-headed reduction of images to language. "My overarching conviction is that we [imagists] bring, and must continue to bring, something special and distinctive to the humanities and the sciences" (Stafford 1991: 6) — a conviction still apt in the era of cognitive linguistics. And again: "In uncovering this ambiguous realm of artful science — lying somewhere between entertainment and information, pleasure and learning — I wish to move past the nihilism of postmodernism with its text-based epistemology" (Stafford 1994: xxiv–xxv).

This struggle maps across a series of books exploring the constitutive, not the illustrative, role of images in the sciences (from geology to biology). At issue was how to make science humanistically relevant and not reductive while making the visual humanities less driven by competing methodologies and more by exciting new data. Along the way, I argued that not all visual media do the same thing but diversely perform and differentially externalize mental work. As enactors, they are central to cognition and not just purveyors of illusion — a fact all the more important to understand today as Internet cultures are reshaping the neuroplastic brain.

2. The Visible Invisible

I believe the single most significant development for the field (and for the humanities and social sciences in general) is the emerging confluence between questions coming from the humanities/social science side of imaging with those coming from the developing brain sciences. Research areas that humanists routinely thought were their own: the imagination, perception, memory, and creativity are being looked at anew, from the inside out. I think it opens up collaborative research opportunities as well as forcing us to reframe our fundamental definitions. Conversely, it demonstrates why the neurosciences need the humanities to adequately frame their notions of mirroring, affect — even of image itself.

3. A Philosophy of the Senses

So what is still valuable in my earlier books — examining the multifarious intersections of the historical arts and sciences specifically with regard to their distinctive deployment of the visual modality — given the new and exciting research emerging from the brain sciences? Making the unseen seen and expressible underlies neuroscientific investigations looking at how different sensory modalities (i.e., visual, auditory, tactile, olfactory, gustatory sensations) are actually different styles of exploring the world. Even disorienting visions, hallucinations, or dreams deploy our sensorimotor mechanisms to imagine things that we do not face, explore what we cannot see directly, and experience what is happening behind, below, or above us. Not surprisingly, philosophical dualism has become a rare epistemology since psychological or psychogenic phenomena are increasingly seen as the monistic effects, or elusive qualia, of a material organ.

Further, the discovery of the systematic interconnectedness of the visual with the motor cortex so that perceptual consciousness varies as a function of movement in relation to the environment (already foreseen by J.J. Gibson) amplifies the ancient dialectic between the visible and the invisible. The literal as well as the metaphorical problem of how we get from where one is to where one is not continues to be a coordinating challenge. Hence the study of human and animal consciousness has become phenomenologically more complex, operating as an embodied, embedded, and distributed performative process not statically localized in brain modules but extending outward into the ambient. On one hand, because of the synaptic cleft separating discrete neurons, fragmented brain structure can be likened to a Matisse cutout. On the other hand, because of cross-cortical parallel processing, it can give rise to Rothko-like seepages and blending color fields.

4. The Desire to Connect

Emotion as the permeating "feeling of what happens" (think of it as e[motion]) appears to be interactively connected with all perception — except when its empathetic mirroring powers are thwarted or broken (as in Autism, Asperger syndrome, or ADD). Mirroring, or intuitive form-finding in another being's face and gestures, also lies at the heart of an ancient theory of physiognomic and pathognomic participation. If reflective empathy or social outreach is an artifact of adaptive evolution shared by animals from rats to primates, then it is also the biological root of similitude-seeking or bond-making analogy: "the mimetic vocabulary of similarity and dissimilarity" (Stafford 1999: 2–3). And again: "The capacity to exchange intimate perspectives in real time reminds us of the truth of William James's aphorism, 'Thinking is for doing'" (James quoted in Stafford 2011: 28).

Consequently, not just the potentialities of our body but its constraints — those oppositions and contraries needing to be reconciled — plus the divisive spatial dimensionality of the world (requiring constant reorientation, redirection, recalibration), effectively set the rules by which we judge our surroundings and relate to each other. The appeal of metaphors, or cross-domain mappings, speaks to this desire to associate, to craft linkages that are more than arbitrary or merely idiosyncratic. Recent research shows that even among synaesthetes, where idiosyncrasy is the rule, commonalities emerge.

5. The New Formalism

Similarly, saliency, bilateral symmetry, shade, contour, and edge perception, vertical/horizontal/diagonal vectors, color blocking, and optical illusions constitute the skeletal elements of a rule-based art. For numerous late-eighteenth and early-nineteenth century thinkers, the unconditional line became the basic component with which to establish the longed-for objective correlative between an inner world of sensibility and an outer world of impersonal objects (Stafford 1979). Recent work on pattern generation and pattern recognition — repeat patterns, grids, arabesques, diagrams, geometrical motifs — indicates that no ornament is merely "ornamental." "Decorative" design originates in cognitive mechanisms whereby the brain sets certain conditions for the organization of visual perception. We pay more acute attention to stripped down, minimalist, austere performances that correspond to our internal ordering systems.

Stating the issue in artistic terms is to blast open the formal design logic of composition, construction, and genre typologies. To be sure social factors contribute to the creation and reception of any cultural artifact (taken up in the case made for a Neural Darwinism and the shaping of what Gerald Edelman terms the secondary repertoire). But the "how" of that societal influence, I believe, needs to be reformulated just as we also need to devise a new formalism — one not afraid to look at cultural surfaces from the bottom up and inside out. The neurosciences provide new ways for understanding the meaningfulness of cognitively easeful (smooth gradient forms) or effortful visual formats such as mosaics, emblems, collage/montage — indeed of any conspicuously patterned ensemble.

6. Arriving at Attention

From the vantage of hindsight, I think all my work ultimately revolves around the complex relationship between the varieties of everyday as well as heightened attention and the reflective or unreflective registration of visual stimuli. The seeing act or "acts of matter" range from fleeting glimpse, to glance, to occasional noticing, to scanning, to roving gaze, to sustained foveal attention. Perceptual consciousness is intrinsically performative: either largely involuntary (stemming from a brain whose mechanisms are surmised to be approximately 90% autonomous, autopoietic), or, to a much lesser degree, voluntary (resulting from effort, training, expertise [a paltry 10% of brain function]). Thus the question of the relationship between pre-selective (spontaneous, intuitive reaction) and selective (cognitively labor-intensive framing) or "willed" seeing becomes acute (Stafford 1984).

Consequently, I believe the single most important issue to be addressed by the field today is the vanishing of mindful attentiveness, discernment, the awareness that we are aware (endogenous control) from spectator response. The spread of filtering devices and surveillance apparatuses, the enthralling hold of computer gaming on adolescents, the common advertising use of covert targeted marketing, has rendered the problem of conscious versus unconscious attention critical. Further, as I argued in *Echo Objects: The Cognitive Work of Images* (Stafford 2007), the exponential growth in digital devices specifically targeting the brain's reward systems urgently calls us to address the explosion of automatically generated, contextless images littering the twenty-first century: apps, PDAs, iPhones.

Designing for the Future: What sort of higher-order images make us attend to another human being, a situation, an event, the life world? What kinds of images do we need to design to thwart autopilot? What can the history of images and art bring to the table as models, templates to counteract the power of external stimuli (exogenous control) that override any operative attentional state and direct it elsewhere? How can we begin to enrich impoverished conceptions of experience dependent on knee-jerk reactions with images that contribute to an active and meaning-driven construction of the world around us and not just to a virtual reality?

Selected publications by Barbara Maria Stafford

1979. *Symbol and Myth: Humbert de Superville's Essay on Absolute Signs in Art*. Cranbury: University of Delaware.

1984. *Voyage into Substance: Art, Science and the Illustrated Travel Account, 1760-1840*. Cambridge: MIT Press.

1991. *Body Criticism: Imaging the Unseen in Enlightenment Art and Medicine*. Cambridge: MIT Press.

1994. *Artful Science: Enlightenment Entertainment and the Eclipse of Visual Education*. Cambridge: MIT Press.

1999. *Visual Analogy: Consciousness as the Art of Connecting*. Cambridge: MIT Press.

2001. *Devices of Wonder: From the World in a Box to Images on a Screen*. Los Angeles: Getty Publications.

2007. *Echo Objects: The Cognitive Work of Images*. Chicago: University of Chicago Press.

2011. *A Field Guide to a New Meta-field: Bridging the Humanities-Neurosciences Divide*. Chicago: University of Chicago Press.

19

Felix Thürlemann

Professor in Art History at the University of Konstanz

---

1. Why were you initially drawn to the study of images?

I grew up in a rural area near St. Gallen, Switzerland, and images happened to be a natural part of my world: a few of them, an old oil painting and photos of deceased relatives, were hanging in the living room, others were found as illustrations in children books. Yet, most important were the big paintings and frescos over the altars and ceilings of the baroque village church. These images were – in virtue of their historic distance and their reference to fact I was not always familiar with – oftentimes incomprehensible. But it was exactly because of their enigmatic character and rhetoric ardour that they became appreciated companions in hours of enforced boredom.

I was nearsighted and had been wearing glasses from early on. The glasses could be put away – and then the world looked differently, and by no means worse. The colours now appeared stronger, almost impressionistically autonomous. Via a small manipulation I was able to see them as I *wanted* them to see. Thus, seeing itself had become subject of reflection.

When, after attending a high-school that was stuffed with especially bad images, I came to the University of Zürich, I went to a lecture in art history upon the advice of my girlfriend. After just a few minutes I fell asleep. The quality of the lecture was less to blame than the fact that lights had to be switched off because of the dias. Thus, I stuck with the three philological subjects: French language and literature, medieval Latin and Latin literature.

After a few study semesters a new professor took over the chair in French literature: Jacques Geninasca. In his seminars I had learned the pivotal thing for my academic development: Namely, that meaning is not given, but rather has to always result from a concrete shaping of form and has to be reconstructed in an intensive, method-driven reflection as a scientific subject of study. In these literature seminars, images had been already present implicitly. Not only, because Geninasca was trained as a painter and had a special sense for the laws of composition;

we dealt with *Les Chimères* by Gérard de Nerval in the first semester, a collection of especially hermetic sonnets. These language images could – this was key to their interpretation – be viewed as diagrams. With the conventionalized strophic order, they were showing the reader which words and phrases had to be correlated to let sense arise in a well-ordered interplay.

The next stop was Paris, where I, after this preparation in structuralist readings, enrolled in the seminar of Algirdas Julien Greimas at the Ecole Pratique of the Hautes Etudes en Sciences Sociales. Back then, Greimas, the grand strategist of collective research, was – after he had developed his semiotic model out of the narrative structure of folk tales – not much interested in text analysis anymore. Images, dance, music and gestural language were now to be conquered in a mutual effort for semiotics as a general theory of meaning (not as theory of signs as described by the American "enemy" Charles Sanders Peirce). As I one day sat in the monkishly furnished cell in the Maison Suisse, built by Le Corbusier, in the Cité universitaire international, and once again turned my eyes to a postcard reproduction of Paul Klee's water colour *Blumen Mythos* (again the creation of an exiled Swiss!), I told myself: Why not try, even with such an object, to apply what I had learned by means of the sonnets of Gerard de Nerval beforehand and what Greimas had developed as a general means of meaning analysis in his treatise *Sémantique structural*. I got to work. "C'est bon, mais ..." – "That is o.k. but ..." was Greimas unforgettable first sentence, after he had read my first attempt in visual semiotics. Encouragement, followed by merciless criticism – I knew there was still much to do. With *Paul Klee – analyse sémiotique de trois peintures*, I finally received my doctorate. Thus, in the end I had become an art historian.

Important was, after this new step, my two year stay at the Swiss Institute in Rome. The visits of the Roman churches, monuments and museums, the excursions into southern Italy that I mostly undertook along with a painter, Rolf Winnewisser, became a seeing school that I still feed upon to this day.

2. What do you consider your contribution to the field?

In my earlier works I tried – alongside colleagues such as Jean Marie Floch – according to the principles of European semiotics (i.e. in line of traditional Ferdinand de Saussure – Louis Hjelmslev – Algirdas Julien Greimas) to analyse individual objects of modern contemporary western image culture (works by Paul Klee, Wassily Kandinsky, or Bruce Nauman), in each case self-contained carriers of meaning, as visual texts. The aim was, parallel to practical analysis, to develop a universally applicable instruments in order to include images as important, formerly neglected objects of inquiry into the semiotic project. In doing so, contributions from color analysis over the physiognomic dimension of meaning and to visual narratology emerged. Later I also more and more turned to older works, paintings by Nicolas Poussin and Albrecht Dürer or examples of architecture by Francesco Borromini; and finally to the complete pictorial works of Robert Campin, the so-called master of Flémalle. Here, important elements of the relevant historic aesthetics had to be reconstructed in the process as a source for understanding, for instance, the theory of the passions, as it is central for understanding 17th century painting. The originally ahistoric access to images had thus been complemented with a cultural-historical dimension, whose retrieval had to obey not only the usual philological, but also the semiotic principles of meaning reconstruction.

Three phenomena have been added in recent times as focus of research: diagrams, cartography and what I call 'hyperimage'. These proved to be highly related. The original constraint of visual semiotics on the analysis of individual works – mostly popular works in visual arts – was, considering the stage of development back then, justified to a certain extent but did not live up to the general way in which images are created, manipulated and perceived in society. The image appears in the real world usually in combination with other works, as image in the plural. This is not only the case in museum presentations, but also in diverse forms of media distribution, in the illustrated art book, e.g., and more recently on the internet.

That the image had been used "in the plural" in the past already, however, was shown by Wolfgang Kemp in his trend-setting studies of medieval image systems. In order to account for the image in the plural in recent forms of appearance I coined the concept of 'hyperimage' by analogy to *hypertext*. This term signifies that the changing arrangements of per se autonomous works through the curator and designer cannot be described as mere summations, but must be understood, again, as works of higher order themselves. As examples, take a museum wall arranged according to the pendant principle or the double pages in Wölfflin's *Kunstgeschichtliche Grundbegriffe* with their coupled presentations of illustrations. What is special and especially interesting about hyperimages is that they have the status of meta-discourses in relation to the works they are composed of. The respective neighborhoods provoke, by the perception of a selected work, comparative seeing and lead, through the recognition of similarities and differences, to the formation of significant categories for the reception of the work. Thus, the art collection, in which the stock of European pictorial art from the 17th century and far into the 20th century is presented in hierarchized and symmetric orders, the so-called pendant-hanging [in German: "Pendant-Hängung], prove powerful instruments of the intellectualizing of art. Since hyperimage structures operate in the act of perception itself, they are particularly efficient instruments in the interpretation of the concerned works.

Hyperimages manifest themselves in space and can thus be considered as large diagrams. Hence, the second branch of research, with which I have dealt in recent times, is indicated: Diagrammatics, in whose exploration my dialogue with Steffen Bogen from Universität Konstanz plays a crucial role. Diagrams can be defined as visual texts in the wider sense, where content categories, according to the mode of semi-symbolic meaning production, are connected to visual categories (for instance, those of spatial orientation such as left/right, up/down, front/back, or colour contrasts, etc.). The integration of linguistic terms, as it is the case in the tradition of the 'lettered diagram', is not necessary to determine the diagram. Additionally, it is appropriate not only to speak of the diagram as an image form, but also of the diagrammatic as a general mode of meaning production that extends from scientific discourse into social practice. When, in a village church, women were previously seated on the right and men on the left side, this counts as a manifestation of the diagrammatic. Also countless works of the fine arts rely, especially when they make a general, cosmological claim, intensively on the diagrammatic mode of meaning. Thus, for instance, the famous glass painting *Duccio* created in the year 1287 for the Siena cathedral, is as much a diagram as a complex image ensemble. For a rational analysis of images Diagrammatics takes a central role.

Most recently, research into cartography, which I also undertook together with Steffen Bogen, has eventually taken an important place. The aim of these investigations – for instance, considering the example of the city maps of Rome – was to understand maps in their respective function, as instruments allowing the client, illustrator, and user to orient themselves in the world, to rule and change it.

3. What is the proper role of the study of images in relation to other academic disciplines?

Images of all kind were first deployed by the sciences in an instrumental role, as means of argumentation and illustration. Only European art history, as it established itself in the 19th century– beside philosophy, which merely commented on art on a general level, i.e. on the aesthetic dimension of images – made them into a proper subject of critical analysis. Art history initially limited itself to the study of inherited historic monuments and the so-called *Kunstbilder*, as they had been collected in the great museums and whose actual purpose was thought to be aesthetic pleasure. The important, artistically valuable images were supposedly all without purpose. When it became standard practice to describe their content according to the rules of iconography, it served only, at first, the identification of the represented object, which mostly equaled the identification of the so-called written 'source'. As a complement to iconography, dealing with 'content', the history of styles investigated – most often radically separated from the former – 'form' in its changing conventional occurences. This division of labour between a content and a form analysis was questioned at the latest by modernity. Numerous scholars, such as Hans Sedlmayr or Max Imdahl, developed new methodological approaches on the pinncale of abstract art in order to explain the production of meaning out of the concrete configuration of the visual substance. Visual semiotics was able to continue and make more precise these approaches.

Two incidents in particular have been important for the development of a new interest in images outside of the constraints of the art system: the late, but intensive reception of the writings of Aby Warburg since the 1960's and the parallel proclamation of the 'iconic turn' or 'pictorial turn', respectively, by G. Boehm and W. J. T. Mitchell in the year 1994. Unlike the movement of the linguistic turn, which the terminology mirrored, the iconic/pictorial turn could not refer to an already existing framework. The formula was a pure battle cry articulating the new interest developing in society for images of all kinds, due to the digital revolution. Therefore, it came as no surprise when the postulated 'science of images' was given various names and was institutionally integrated in different ways. The American 'visual studies' primarily orient themselves toward sociology and media studies, while the German 'Bildwissenschaft' (image science) draws its terminology and elements of methodology out of philosophy and art history. Both additionally regularly refer to semiotics, although rarely in a systematic way.

Through the introduction of cultural-historical and image-scientific problems, art history has gained a new status. Its relationship to a science of images, in its core still to be developed, is ambivalent. It must not give up its classical subjects, but is prompted to define these in their special structure within the general field of image practice and reconstruct them in their special historic usages. Without a defined corpus of images (such as culture images, traditional art images or illustrations of technical treatises, geographical maps, or diagrams) the science of images remains "anemic", while art history conversely remains without orientation towards general image-scientific and semiotic problems in a blind reflection-less practice. The interplay of systematic reflection and concrete, historically founded meaning analysis is central to the examination of images – whichever disciplinary integration one might choose for it.

4. What do you consider the most important topics and/or contributions in the study of images?

There have been attempts to develop a general image science out of problematics and methodological approaches of existing scientific disciplines. For instance, philosophical aesthetics, rhetorics, Gestalt psychology, and psychology of perception have served as frames of reference. However, such transfers necessarily come up short. In my eyes only a 'semiotic hypothesis', i.e. the assumption that meaning results from specifically formed visual substances, can provide a basis for future general image theory. If pragmatics, the question of the usage of images, is thereby moved to the centre of interest, it will be possible additionally to equip the semiotic approach with a 'historic consciousness', in order to investigate the diverse accomplishments of images in alternating social contexts. General image theory and historic image analysis do not have to exclude each other.

5. What are the most important open problems in this field and what are the prospects/avenues for progress?

The challenge for a future image science/visual studies are not just of methodological nature. It is the sheer mass and diversity of images that let any general discourse about images appear risky and problematic. I consider the question 'What is an image?' dangerous, when is thereby suggested the possibility of a general identification for all forms of visual communication. The world of images is extremely diverse and complex, more diverse even than the world of natural languages. In my eyes, questions concerning the shifting functions of single image types in specific pragmatic contexts are more profitable than the question concerning the image in singular, which is bound to lead to impermissible reifications. Questions like the following I deem fruitful: What do single image types achieve within a specific culture, why were they created and used, what do diagrams achieve, why are they efficient? How were images used before and how are they now used as a means for political incapacitation or liberation, respectively? Or: How were geographical maps used before and how are they used today? What consequences does digitalization have for individual traditional image forms? For example: How did geographical maps change, whether they can, as a result of digitalization, be personalized by the user in various ways and be exploited by providers as an advertising medium and therefore implicitly mutate from a means of orientation to a means of manipulation.

Extensive problem areas which remain to this day insufficiently clarified comprehend, for instance, the relationship between static and moving images or the questions of hypermedia links between individual sensory channels and different technical media. These questions cannot be assessed anymore with old formulas like 'ut picture poesis' or 'images as bible for the illiterate' in a reasonable way. A big problem which has so far been barely addressed: The focalization of the 'image' – particularly inherent in the German term 'Bildwissenschaft' – can further strengthen the inadequate privileging of the 2-d image – painting, photography, the ones appearing on every kind of screen. Classical art studies had the possibility, with the triad of the sister disciplines painting, sculpture and architecture, to focus on the spatial reference of any visual appearance in a systematic way. The study of images should therefore always be the study of space, as well.

The current enthusiasm for image-scientific problems should be beneficial in two ways: for the precise investigation of detail and at the same time for the striving of ordering the image field in its diversity, perhaps less to partition it into individual disciplines, but rather to give particular research a frame of thought. Old art history, as the so far most advanced science of images, will have to play a double paradoxical role in the process: Due to the knowledge about historic image forms and image usages deposited in it, it can provide fully developed methodological instruments for image-scientific research; however, as a science of traditional art forms with a very delimited range, it simultaneously has to orient itself toward a general image-scientific framework. Image science/visual studies and art history mutually complement one another and may develop, in a productive dialogue, a science of images that lives up to the central role of visual communication in contemporary society.

Translation: Jonas Nölle

Selected publications by Felix Thürlemann

1982. *Paul Klee: analyse sémiotique de trois peintures*, Lausanne: L'Age d'Homme.

1979. "Die Farbe in der Malerei: symbolischer und semi-symbolischer Bedeutungsmodus." In: *Semiotics Unfolding: Proceedings of the Second Congress of the International Association for Semiotic Studies*, vol, 3, edited by Tasso Borbé,1389-1396. Vienna-Den Haag: Mouton.

1983. "The Function of Admiration in the Esthetic of the XVIIth Century." In: *Paris School Semiotics*, vol. II. edited by A.J. Greimas et al., 43-65. Toronto, Victoria University: Practice (= Toronto Semiotic Circle Monographs 4).

1985. "Le mode de signification 'immédiat' ou physionomique." In: *Exigences et perspectives de la sémiotique: recueil d'hommages pour A.J. Greimas*, edited by H. Parret and H.-G. Ruprecht, vol. II, 661-669. Amsterdam: John Benjamins.

1986. *Kandinsky über Kandinsky: der Künstler als Interpret eigener Werke*. Bern: Benteli.

1989. "Fictionality in Mantegna's San Zeno Altarpiece: Structures of Mimesis and the History of Painting." *New Literary History* 20, 747-761.

1990. *Vom Bild zum Raum: Beiträge zu einer semiotischen Kunstwissenschaft*. Cologne: DuMont.

2002. *Robert Campin. A Monograph with Critical Catalogue*. Munich/ New York: Prestel.

2003 (with Steffen Bogen). "Jenseits der Opposition von Text und Bild: Überlegungen zu einer Theorie des Diagramms und des Diagrammatischen." In: *Die Bildwelt der Diagramme Joachims von Fiore: zur Medialität religiös-politischer Programme im Mittelalter*, edited by Alexander Patschovsky, Stuttgart: Thorbecke, 1-22.

2004. "Vom Einzelbild zum ‚hyperimage': eine neue Herausforderung für die kunstgeschichtliche Hermeneutik." In: *Les herméneutiques au seuil du XXIème siècle – évolution et débat actuel*, edited by Ada Neschke-Hentschke, Leuwen/ Paris, 223-247.

2005. "Bild gegen Bild: für eine Theorie des vergleichenden Sehens." In: *Zwischen Literatur und Anthropologie – Diskurse, Medien, Performanzen*, edited by Aleida Assmann, Ulrich Gaier und Gisela Trommsdorff, Tübingen, 163-174.

2009. (With Steffen Bogen) *Rom. Eine Stadt in Karten von der Antike bis heute*, Primus Verlag, Darmstadt 2009.

2010 (with David Ganz) (eds.). *Das Bild im Plural: mehrteilige Bildformen zwischen Mittelalter und Gegenwart*. Berlin: Reimer.

2011. "The Paradoxical Rhetoric of Tears: Looking at the Madrid *Descent from the Cross*." In: *Crying in the Middle Ages: Tears of History*, editd by Elina Gertsman, New York/ London: Routledge.

20

Kendall L. Walton

Professor Emeritus at the University of Michigan

---

1. Why were you initially drawn to the study of images?

I came to aesthetics from music. But I immediately found myself seriously immersed in, almost obsessed by, philosophical questions about the visual arts. Why, I am not sure. But I think I have always been intrigued by pictures (still images more than film), fascinated by them in a way that I don't quite understand. My experience snapping photographs in my youthful wanderings had something to do with it, but was perhaps more an effect than a cause of my fascination.

Once I started thinking about images I realized that it is not at all easy to understand how they work and why they are as important in our lives as they obviously are. Neither philosophers nor psychologists had, by then, paid much attention to images (this has changed in the last decade or two). Thinking of pictures on the model of linguistic symbols — as symbols that are such by virtue of resemblance, for instance, rather than convention, but which function otherwise much like linguistic symbols — seemed to me, and still does, unhelpful and unilluminating. There was a huge vacuum. I was hooked.

My philosophical interest in pictures preceded and inspired my interest in fiction. I was preoccupied initially with the puzzle of what is especially *visual* about pictorial representations in contrast to words, given that we use our eyes to read (written) words as we do to understand and appreciate pictures. Ernst Gombrich's examples convinced me that pictorial representation as well as language involves something like convention. And I took from Goodman not the idea that resemblances have nothing to do with depiction, but rather that what kinds of resemblances are involved and what role they play is seriously problematic. The solution, I decided, consists in recognizing the role of pictures in what I call visual games of make-believe. Working this idea out required and inspired developing my make-believe theory of fiction.

2. What do you consider your contribution to the field?

I like to think that I have made two main contributions: One is my account of pictures as props in visual games of make-believe — my solution to the puzzle about the visual-ness of pictorial representation, which is central also in my thoughts about how pictures function as well as how and why they are important. Actually not just pictures but also sculptures, film, theatrical, and dance performances are props in visual games of make-believe.

The account is easily generalized to include the more obvious kinds of musical representation as well. It is absolutely crucial that we recognize what all of these *depictive* representations have in common, notwithstanding the obvious differences among them. Too often, attempts to understand pictures focus narrowly on pictures alone, and so fail to capture what is really basic about them, what they share with other members of the larger genus, as opposed to what differentiates the species from one another. A decision to restrict the scope of one's investigation sounds innocent enough. Yes, life is short. But in this case and many others, a narrow focus limits and impoverishes one's understanding of what one is focusing on. To understand what is *visual* about pictorial representation is to see what pictures have in common with depictions, perceptual representations of many other kinds, and how depictions differ from, e.g., literary representations. The make-believe account of pictures also enables us to understand them and experiences of them as related, more distantly, to a wide variety of other objects and activities, including literary fictions, children's make-believe games, many computer games, and even certain non-literal uses of language (metaphor, irony) — all of which involve one or another variety of make-believe in one way or another. Once we realize this, we have resources for understanding the large and small differences among these various objects and activities. Make-believe activities differ in many ways. Some are visual or partly visual, others are not; some are established and widely recognized, others local, temporary, and/or ad hoc — often introduced for special purposes. People participate in various make-believe activities in different ways: deliberately or spontaneously, automatically, consciously or unconsciously, publicly or privately, extensively or minimally. Many of the details about various kinds of cases remain to be worked out, but tools for explaining a wide variety of human experiences and activities, prominently including picture perception, are in place.

The other main contribution I like to claim, with respect to images, is my account of the difference between photographic and hand-made pictures, which is naturally expressed by saying that to see a photograph is actually to *see*, indirectly, the photographed objects. Photographs (ordinary snapshots, at least) are "transparent," I say, whereas paintings and drawings are not. Like mirrors and telescopes, photographs are aids to vision, enabling us to see things that we could not see without them. Photographic pictures also serve as props in visual games of make-believe, as paintings and drawings do. So they have a fascinating dual function. Think of photographs that are pictures of and photographs of different things: Some *photographs* of Judy Garland are *pictures* of Dorothy in the land of Oz.

Many have claimed that the difference between photographs and hand made pictures is epistemological, that photographs provide more and better evidence for what they portray than other kinds of pictures do. This is often true, but needn't be, and it is not the most important difference between them. Seeing — ordinary, direct, face-to-face seeing — does not always tell us much about what we see; sometimes we don't even realize what it is that we are seeing. And we often learn a lot about things that we do not see, frequently from hand-made pictures of them. The fact that we see things via photographs is itself enormously important, apart from what we might thereby learn about them. And this distinguishes photographs (snapshots anyway) sharply from paintings and drawings.

Selected publications by Kendall L. Walton

1973/2008. "Pictures and Make-Believe." *The Philosophical Review* July: 283–319. Reprinted in *Marvelous Images: On Values and the Arts*. New York: Oxford University Press.

1990. *Mimesis As Make-Believe: On the Foundations of the Representational Arts*. Cambridge: Harvard University Press.

2008a. *Marvelous Images: On Values and the Arts*. New York: Oxford University Press.

2008b. "Transparent Pictures." In *Marvelous Images: On Values and the Arts*. New York: Oxford University Press.

2008c."Experiencing Still Photographs: What Do You See and How Long Do You See It?" In *Marvelous Images: On Values and the Arts*. New York: Oxford University Press.

2012. "Fotografische Bilder." In Julian Nida-Rümelin & Jakob Steinbrenner, eds., *Fotografie zwischen Dokmentation und Inszenierung*. Ostfildern: Hatje Cantz Verlag.

About the Editors

Aud sissel Hoel is Professor of Media Studies and Visual Culture at the Norwegian University of Science and Technology. Her research focuses on the roles of images and visual tools in knowledge and thinking, including photography, scientific images, medical imaging and visualisation. Hoel's publications cover a wide range of topics in the overlapping fields of visual studies, science studies and media philosophy.

Peer Bundgaard is Associate Professor in Cognitive Semiotics at Aarhus University. He is the editor in chief of the journal *Cognitive Semiotics*. Bundgaard has published articles in journals such as *Synthese, Phenomenology and the Cognitive Sciences, Semiotica,* and *Cognitive Semiotics*, and recently he edited *Investigations into the Phenomenology and the Ontology of the Work of Art* (with F. Stjernfelt, 2015).

Frederik Stjernfelt is Professor of Semiotics, Intellectual History and Theory of Science at the Aalborg University Copenhagen. He is the co-director of the Humanomics Research Center, Aalborg University Copenhagen. Stjernfelt has published, among other things, *Diagrammatology* (2007), *Democratic Contradictions of Multiculturalism* (with J.-M. Eriksen, 2012), and *Natural Propositions* (2014).

Bibliography

Alphen, Ernst van. 2005. *Art in Mind: How Contemporary Images Shape Thought*. Chicago: University of Chicago Press.

D'Angiulli, Amedeo, John M. Kennedy, and Morton A. Heller. 1998. "Blind Children Recognizing Tactile Pictures Respond like Sighted Children Given Guidance in Exploration." *Scandinavian Journal of Psychology* 39(3): 189-90.

Appadurai, Arjun. 2000. "Grassroot Globalization and the Research Imagination." *Public Culture* 12(1): 1-19.

— 1999. "Globalization and the Research Imagination." *International Social Science Journal* 160: 229-38.

— 1997. "The Research Ethic and the Spirit of Internationalism." *Items* 51(4): Part I: 55-60.

Bal, Mieke. 2013a. *Endless Andness: The Politics of Abstraction According to Ann Veronica Janssens*. London: Bloomsbury.

— 2013b. *Thinking in Film: The Politics of Video Installation According to Eija-Liisa Ahtila*. London: Bloomsbury

— 2010. *Of What One Cannot Speak: Doris Salcedo's Political Art*. Chicago, IL: University of Chicago Press.

— 2009. *Fragments of Matter: Jeannette Christensen*. Bergen: Bergen National Academy of the Arts.

— 2008. *Balthus: Works and Interview*. Barcelona: Ediciones Polígrafa.

— 2002. *Travelling Concepts in the Humanities: A Rough Guide*. Toronto: University of Toronto Press.

— 2001. *Louise Bourgeois' Spider: The Architecture of Artwriting*. Chicago, IL: University of Chicago Press.

— 1999. *Quoting Caravaggio: Contemporary Art, Preposterous History*. Chicago: University of Chicago Press.

— 1997. *The Mottled Screen: Reading Proust Visually*. Translated by A.-L. Milne. Stanford: Stanford University Press.

— 1996. *Double Exposures: The Subject of Cultural Analysis*. London and New York: Routledge.

— 1991 [1994]. *Reading "Rembrandt": Beyond the Word-Image Opposition* [2nd edition]. Cambridge and New York: Cambridge University Press.

— 1988a. *Death and Dissymmetry: The Politics of Coherence in the Book of Judges*. Chicago: University of Chicago Press.

— 1988b. "The Rape of Narrative and the Narrative of Rape: Speech Acts and Body Language in Judges." In *Selected Papers from the English Institute*, edited by E. Scarry, 1-32. Baltimore: Johns Hopkins University Press.

Bal, Mieke, and Michelle Williams Gamaker. 2013. "Scenography of Death: Figuration, Focalization, and Finding Out." *Performance Research* 18(3): 179-86.

Bal, Mieke, and Miguel Á. Hernández-Navarro. 2008. *2MOVE: Video, Art, Migration*. Murcia: Cendeac.

Baxandall, Michael. 1987. *Patterns of Intention: On the Historical Explanation of Pictures*. New Haven: Yale University Press.

— 1972. *Painting and Experience in Fifteenth Century Italy*. Oxford: Oxford University Press.

Baxandall, Michael, and Svetlana Alpers. 1994. *Tiepolo and the Pictorial Intelligence*. New Haven: Yale University Press.

Bender, John, and Michael Marrinan. 2010. *The Culture of Diagram*. Stanford: Stanford University Press.

Benjamin, Walter. 1963. "Das Kunstwerk im Zeitalter seiner technischen Reproduzierbarkeit [1936]." In: *Das Kunstwerk im Zeitalter seiner technischen Reproduzierbarkeit: Drei Studien zur Kunstsoziologie*. Frankfurt: Suhrkamp.

Bennett, Tony, and John Frow, eds. 2008. *The SAGE Handbook of Cultural Analysis*. London: SAGE Publications.

Berry, Ian, Darby English, Vivian Patterson, and Mark Reinhardt, eds. 2003. Kara Walker, *Narratives of a Negress*. Cambridge, Mass.: MIT Press.

Böhme, Gernot. 2011. "Die Kunst des Bühnenbildes als Paradigma einer Ästhetik der Atmosphären." In: *Inszenierung und Vertrauen: Grenzgänge der Szenographie*, edited by R. Bohn and H. Wilharm, 109-17. Bielefeld: Transcript.

— 2007. "Dunstbilder." In: *Das unendliche Kunstwerk: Von der Bestimmtheit des Unbestimmten in der ästhetischen Erfahrung*, edited by G. Gamm and E. Schürmann, 235-48. Hamburg: EVA.

— 2006a. "Körper, Bilder und Gewalt." In: Katalog zur Ausstellung *Annegret Soltau – ich selbst*, edited by K. Schmidt, 152-57. Darmstadt: Mathildenhöhe.

— 2006b. "Nach-Bilder: Zum historischen ort von Neo Rauchs Gemälden." In: *Neo Rauch: Neue Rollen: Bilder 1993-2006*, edited by G. Boehm and G. Böhme, 47-50. Kunstmuseum Wolfsburg. Köln: DuMont.

——2006c. "Die Wirklichkeit der Bilder und ihr Gebrauch." *JTLA, Journal of the Faculty of Letters* 31: 1-12.

——2004a. "Archäologie der Natur in den Materialbildern von Fritz Vahle." In: *Medien Experiment Spiel: Festschrift für Fridhelm Klein*, edited by S. Kretschmer and S. Graupner, 252-69. Wolnzach: Kastner.

——2004b. "Das Bild und sein Medium." In: *Die Medien der Kunst: Die Kunst der Medien*, edited by G. J. Lischka and P. Weibel, 40-65. Wabern: Benteli.

——2004c. "Die Wirklichkeit der Bilder." In: *Media Synaesthetics*, edited by C. Filk, M. Lommel, and M. Sandbothe, 84-94. Köln: Herbert von Halem.

——2003. "Die Wörter und die Bilder bei Magritte." In: *Die Medien der Künste: Beiträge zur Theorie des Darstellens*, edited by D. Mersch, 117-25. München: Fink.

——2001. "Ist die Realität wirklich? Die Bilderwelt gehört zum menschlichen Lebenszusammenhang." *Neue Zürcher Zeitung*, 19-20 May: 99.

——1999. *Theorie des Bildes*. München: Fink.

——1996a. "Dies Bildnis ist bezaubernd schön..." *der blaue reiter* 3: 69-73.

——1996b. "Das Bild der Dämmerung." In: *Das große stille Bild*, edited by N. Bolz and U. Rüffer, 234-45. München: Fink.

Braun, Marta 2014. "Giacomo Balla, Anton Giulio Bragaglia, and Etienne-Jules Marey." In: *Italian Futurism, 1909-1944: Reconstructing the Universe*, edited by V. Greene, 95-103. New York: Solomon R. Guggenheim Museum.

——2010. *Eadweard Muybridge*. London: Reaktion Press.

——2007. "Aux limites du savoir: 1845-1900; la photographie et les sciences de l'observation." In: *L'Art de la Photographie des origins à nos jours,* edited by A. Gunthert and M. Poivert, 139-79. Paris: Citadelles & Mazenod.

——2005. "Chronophotography: Leaving Traces." In: *Moving Pictures: The Un-Easy Relationship between American Art and Early Film, 1890-1910*, edited by N. Matthews, 90-95. Williamstown: Williams College Museum of Art.

——1992. *Picturing Time: The Work of Etienne-Jules Marey,*

1830-1904. Chicago: University of Chicago Press.

Bredekamp, Horst. 2010. *Theorie des Bildakts: Frankfurter Adorno-Vorlesungen 2007.* Berlin: Suhrkamp.

— 2007. *Galilei der Künstler: der Mond, die Sonne, die Hand.* Berlin: Akademie Verlag.

— 2005. *Darwins Korallen. Die frühen Evolutionsdiagramme und die Tradition der Naturgeschichte.* Berlin: Wagenbach.

— 2004. *Das Fenster der Monade: Gottfried Wilhelm Leibniz' Theater der Natur und Kunst.* Berlin: Akademie Verlag.

— 2000. *Sankt Peter in Rom und das Prinzip der produktiven Zerstörung. Bau und Abbau von Bramante bis Bernini.* Berlin: Wagenbach.

— 1999. *Thomas Hobbes visuelle Strategien. Der Leviathan: Das Urbild des modernen Staates. Werkillustrationen und Portraits.* Berlin: Akademie Verlag.

— 1995. *Repräsentation und Bildmagie der Renaissance als Formproblem.* München: Siemens Stiftung.

— 1993. *Florentiner Fußball: die Renaissance der Spiele.* Berlin: Wagenbach.

— 1993. *Antikensehnsucht und Maschinenglauben. Die Geschichte der Kunstkammer und die Zukunft der Kunstgeschichte.* Berlin: Wagenback.

— 1985. *Vicino Orsini und der Heilige Wald von Bomarzo: ein Fürst als Künstler und Anarchist.* Vol. 1 & 2. Worms: Werner'sche Verlagsgesellschaft.

Brennan, Teresa, and Martin Jay, eds. 1996. *Vision in Context: Historical and Contemporary Perspectives on Sight.* New York: Routledge.

Brown, James Robert. Forthcoming. "Das 'Gedankenexperiment'. Die Diskussion der letzten 25 Jahre." *Deutsche Zeitschrift für Philosophie*, 59.

— 2007a. "Counter Thought Experiments." *Royal Institute of Philosophy Supplement 61*, 82: 155-177.

— 2007b. "Thought Experiments in Science, Philosophy, and Mathematics" *Croatian Journal of Philosophy* 7: 3-27.

— 2007c. "Comments and Replies." *Croatian Journal of Philosophy* 7: 249-268.

— 2005. "Naturalism, Pictures, and Platonic Intuitions." In: *Explanations, Visualizations, and Reasoning Styles in*

Mathematics, edited by P. Mancosu, K. F. Jørgensen, and S. A. Pedersen, 57-73. Dordrecht: Springer.

— 2004a. "Why Thought Experiments Do Transcend Empiricism." In: *Contemporary Debates in the Philosophy of Science*, edited by C. Hitchcock, 23-43. Malden: Blackwell.

— 2004b. "Peeking into Plato's Heaven" *Philosophy of Science* 71: 1126-1138.

— 2003. "Why Empiricism Won't Work." *Proceedings of the Philosophy of Science Association* 2: 271-279.

— 1999 [2008]. *Philosophy of Mathematics: A Contemporary Introduction to the World of Proofs and Pictures* [2nd edition]. London and New York: Routledge.

— 1996, revised 2014. "Thought Experiments" (with Yiftach Fehige). *Stanford Encyclopedia of Philosophy*, http://plato.stanford.edu/entries/thought-experiment/

— 1991a [2010]. *Laboratory of the Mind: Thought Experiments in the Natural Sciences*, [2nd edition]. London: Routledge Second Edition.

— 1991b. "Thought Experiments: A Platonic Account." In: *Thought Experiments in Science and Philosophy*, edited by T. Horowitz and G. Massey, 119-28. Lanham: Rowman & Littlefield.

— 1987. "Einstein's Brand of Verificationism." *International Studies in the Philosophy of Science* 2: 33-54.

— 1986. "Thought Experiments since the Scientific Revolution." *International Studies in the Philosophy of Science* 1: 1-15.

Bruhn, Matthias. 2012. "Pictures of a Higher Order." In: *The Islands of Benoît Mandelbrot: Fractals, Chaos, and the Materiality of Thinking*, edited by N. Samuel, 83-89. New York and New Haven: Yale University Press.

— 2011. "Life Lines: An Art History of Biological Research around 1800." *Studies in History and Philosophy of Science* Part C, 42(4): 368-380.

— 2010. "The Iconology of Power: A European Perspective on Political Imagery." In: *United in Visual Diversity: Images and Counter-Images of Europe*, edited by B. Drechsel and C. Leggewie, 17-33. Innsbruck: Studienverlag.

— 2008. *Das Bild: Theorie, Geschichte, Praxis*. Berlin:

Akademie Verlag.

— 2003. *Bildwirtschaft: Verwaltung und Verwertung der Sichtbarkeit*. Weimar: VDG.

— 2003. "Visualization Services: Stock Photography and the Picture Industry." *Genre: Forms of Discourse and Culture* 36 (3/4): 365-381.

Bruhn, Matthias, and Vera Dünkel. 2008. "The Image as Cultural Technology." In: *Visual Literacy*, edited by J. Elkins, 165-78. New York: Routledge.

Cartwright, Lisa. 1995. *Screening the Body: Tracing Medicine's Visual Culture*. Minneapolis: Minnesota University Press.

Dijck, José van. 2005. *The Transparent Body: A Cultural Analysis of Medical imaging* Seattle: The University of Washington Press.

Doyle, Jennifer. 2013. *Hold it Against Me: Difficulty and Emotion in Contemporary Art*. Durham: Duke University Press.

Dunbar, Robin. 2014. *Human Evolution*. London: Penguin.

Elkins, James. 2011. *What Photography Is*. New York: Routledge.

— 2010. *On Pictures and the Words that Fail Them*. Cambridge: Cambridge University Press.

— 1999a. *The Domain of Images*. Ithaca: Cornell University Press.

— 1999b. *What Painting Is: How to Think about Oil Painting, Using the Language of Alchemy*. New York: Routledge.

Frege, Gottlob. 1879. *Begriffsschrift: eine der arithmetischen nachgebildete Formelsprache des reinen Denkens*. Halle: Louis Nebert.

Freud, Sigmund. 1962 [1930]. *Civilization and its Discontents*. Translated and edited by J. Strachey. New York: Norton.

Gibson, James J. 1986. *The Ecological Approach to Visual Perception*. Hillsdale, NJ: Lawrence Erlbaum.

Gombrich, Ernst 1960. *Art and Illusion: A Study in the Psychology of Pictorial Representation*. New York: Pantheon.

Goodman, Nelson. 1968 [1976]. *Languages of Art* [2nd edition]. Oxford: Oxford University Press.

Groupe μ. 2003. *Figuras, conocimiento, cultura: Ensayos retóricos*. Mexico City: Universidad Nacional Autónoma.

— 1992. *Traité du signe visuel: Pour une rhétorique de l'image*. Paris: Seuil.

— 1980. "Plan d'une rhétorique de l'image." *Kodikas/Code* 3: 249-268.

— 1978. *Collages*. Paris: U.G.E.

— 1977. *Rhétorique de la poésie: Lecture lineaire, lecture tabulaire*. Bruxelles: Complexe.

— 1970. *Rhetorique generale*. Paris: Libraire Larousse.

Hagen, Margaret. 1986. *Varieties of Realism: Geometries of Representational Art*. Cambridge: Cambridge University Press.

Hammad, Sherief, John M. Kennedy, Igor Juricevic, and Shazma Rajani. 2008. "Angle Illusion on a Picture's Surface." *Spatial Vision* 21(3-5): 451-462.

Hebb, Donald O. 1949. *The Organization of Behavior: A Neuropsychological Theory*. New York: Wiley and Sons.

Hernández-Navarro, Miguel Á., ed. 2011. *La Ultima Frontera/ The Last Frontier: Obras de Mieke Bal en colaboración con Michelle Williams Gamaker y otros*. Murcia, Spain: Fundación José García Jiménez.

Hirsch, Marianne. 1999. "Projected Memory: *Holocaust* Photographs in Personal and Public Fantasy." In: *Acts of Memory: Cultural Recall in the Present*, edited by M. Bal, J. Crewe, and L. Spitzer, 3-23. Hanover: University Press of New England.

Hopkins, Robert. 2012. "Factive Pictorial Experience: What is Really Special about Photographs?" *Nous* 46 (4): 709-731.

— 2010a. "Inflected Pictorial Experience: Its Treatment and Significance." In: *Philosophical Perspectives on Depiction*, edited by C. Abell and K. Bantinaki, 151-80. Oxford: Oxford University Press.

— 2010b. "Sculpture and Perspective." *British Journal of Aesthetics* 50(3): 1-17.

— 2008. "What Do We See in Film?" *Journal of Aesthetics and Art Criticism* 66(2): 149-59.

— 2004a. "Pictures, Phenomenology and Cognitive Science." *The Monist*, 86(4): 654-76.

— 2004b. "Painting, Sculpture, Sight and Touch." *British Journal of Aesthetics* 44(2): 149-166.

— 2003. "What Makes Representational Painting Truly Visual?" *Proceedings of the Aristotelian Society Supplementary* LXXVII: 149-167.

— 1998. *Picture, Image and Experience.* Cambridge: Cambridge University Press.

Humboldt, Alexander von. 1811. *Political Essay on the Kingdom of New Spain*, Vol. 1. New York: AMS Press.

Hyman, John. 2013. "Depiction." In: *Philosophy and the Arts*, edited by A. O'Hear. Cambridge: Cambridge University Press.

— 2013. "Voluntariness and Choice." *The Philosophical Quarterly* 63(253): 683-708.

— 2010. "Art and Neuroscience." In: *Beyond Mimesis and Convention: Representation in Art and Science*, edited by R. Frigg and M. Hunter. Dordrecht: Springer.

— 2010. "The Road to Larissa." *Ratio* 23(4): 393-414.

— 2006. *The Objective Eye: Color, Form and Reality in the Theory of Art.* Chicago: University of Chicago Press.

— 2006. "Knowledge and evidence." *Mind* 115(460): 891-916.

— 2005. "Realism and Relativism in the Theory of Art." *Proceedings of the Aristotelian Society* 105(1): 25-53.

— 2005. "What, if Anything, are Colours Relative to?" *Philosophy* 80(4): 475-494.

— 2003. "Pains and Places." *Philosophy* 78(1): 5-24.

— 2001. "-ings and –ers." *Ratio* 14(4): 298-317.

— 1999. "How knowledge works." *The Philosophical Quarterly* 49 (197): 433-451.

Imbert, Claude. 2013. "Boas, de Berlin à New York, manières de vivre, manières de voir." In: *Franz Boas: Le travail du regard*, edited by M. Espagne and I. Kalinowski. Paris: Colin.

— 2010-2011. "La monnaie du regard." *La Part de l'œil* 25/26.

— 2008a. "Le bleu de la mer années 1950." In: *Maurice Merleau-Ponty*, edited by E. de Saint Aubert. Paris: Hermann.

— 2008b. *Lévi-Strauss le passage du Nord-Ouest.* Paris: Herne.

— 2004. "Les droits de l'image." In: *Michel Foucault: La Peinture de Manet.* Paris: Seuil.

— 2003. "Warburg, de Kant à Boas." *L'Homme* 165: 11-40.

— 1971. "Introduction." In : Écrits logiques et philosophiques: Gottlob Frege. Translation and introduction by C. Imbert. Paris: Seuil.

Jay, Martin. 2011. *Essays from the Edge: Parerga and Paralipomena.* Charlottesville: University of Virginia Press.

—— 2009. "Magical Nominalism: Photography and the Reenchantment of the World." *Culture, Theory and Critique* 50 (2-3): 16-183.

——, ed. 2005. *Journal of Visual Culture*, 4(2), special issue: The Current State of Visual Culture Studies.

—— 2003. *Refractions of Violence.* New York: Routledge.

—— 1993. *Downcast Eyes: The Denigration of Vision in Twentieth-Century French Thought.* Berkeley: University of California Press.

—— 1993. *Force Fields: Between Intellectual History and Cultural Critique.* New York and London: Routledge.

Jeannerod, Marc. 1997. *The Cognitive Neuroscience of Action.* Oxford: Blackwell.

Juricevic, Igor, and John M. Kennedy. 2006. "Looking at Perspective Pictures from Too Far, Too Close and Just Right." *Journal of Experimental Psychology: General* 135(3): 448-461.

Kennedy, John M. 2009. "Outline, Mental States and Drawings by a Blind Woman." *Perception* 38(10): 1481-1496.

—— 2003. "Drawings from Gaia, a Blind Girl." *Perception* 32(3): 321-340.

—— 1993. *Drawing and the Blind: Pictures to Touch.* New Haven: Yale University Press.

Kennedy, John M., and Juan Bai. 2004. "Line at Shape-From-Shadow Border Tested with Stereo." *Perception* 33(6): 653-665.

Kennedy, John M., Christopher D. Green, Andrea Nicholls, and Chang Hong Liu. 1992. "Illusions and Knowing What Is Real." *Ecological Psychology* 4(3): 153-172.

Kennedy, John M., and Igor Juricevic. 2006a. "Foreshortening, Convergence and Drawings From a Blind Adult." *Perception*, 35(6): 847-851.

—— 2006b. "Blind Man Draws Using Diminution in Three Dimensions." *Psychonomic Bulletin and Review.* 13(3): 506-509.

Kennedy, John M., and Cynthia Merkas. 2000. "Depictions of Motion Devised by a Blind Person." *Psychonomic Bulletin and Review* 7(4): 700-706.

Kennedy, John M., Marta Wnuczko, Marcelo Santos, Peter Coppin, and Karen Singh. 2011. "Dots, Line, Contour & Surface Edge Trigger Centre-surround Pickup Mechanism." In: *Studies in Perception & Action, Xi: Sixteenth International Conference on Perception and Action*, edited by E. P. Charles and L. J. Smart. New York: Psychology Press.

Klinkenberg, Jean-Marie. 2000. *Précis de sémiotique générale*. Paris: Seuil.

Kugler, Franz. 1842. *Handbuch der Kunstgeschichte*. Stuttgart : Ebner & Seubert.

Leroi-Gourhan, André. 1964-1965. *Le geste et la parole*, 2 Vols. Paris: Albin Michel.

Lévi-Strauss, Claude. 1964-1971. *Mythologiques*, 4 Vols. Paris: Plon.

Lopes, Dominic McIver. 2014. *Beyond Art*. Oxford: Oxford University Press.

—— 2011a. "An Empathic Eye." In: *Empathy: Philosophical and Psychological Perspectives*, edited by P. Goldie and A. Coplan. Oxford: Oxford University Press.

—— 2011b. "The Myth of (Non-Aesthetic) Artistic Value." *Philosophical Quarterly* 61: 518-36.

—— 2009a. *A Philosophy of Computer Art*. London: Routledge.

—— 2009b. "Drawing in a Social Science: Lithic Illustration." *Perspectives on Science* 17: 5-25.

—— 2008. "Nobody Needs a Theory of Art." *Journal of Philosophy* 105: 109-27.

—— 2005. *Sight and Sensibility: Evaluating Pictures*. Oxford: Oxford University Press.

—— 2003a. "Pictures and the Representational Mind." *Monist* 86: 32-52.

—— 2003b. "The Aesthetics of Photographic Transparency." *Mind* 112: 433-48.

—— 1997. "Art Media and the Sense Modalities: Tactile Pictures." *Philosophical Quarterly* 47: 425-40.

—— 1996. *Understanding Pictures*. Oxford: Oxford University Press.

Liu, Chang Hong, and John M. Kennedy. 1997. "Form Symbolism, Analogy and Metaphor." *Psychonomic Bulletin & Review* 4(4): 546-551.

Meltzer, Eve. 2013. *Systems We Have Loved: Conceptual Art, Affect, and the Antihumanist Turn*. Chicago: University of Chicago Press.

Merleau-Ponty, Maurice. 1969. *La prose du monde*. Paris: Gallimard.
Milner, A. David, and Goodale, Melvyn A. 1995. *The Visual Brain in Action*. Oxford: Oxford University Press.
Mitchell, W. J. T. 2012. *Seeing Madness: Insanity, Media, and Visual Culture*. Ostfildern: Hatje Cantz.
— 2011. *Cloning Terror: The War of Images, 9/11 to the Present*. Chicago and London: University of Chicago Press.
— 2005. *What Do Pictures Want?* Chicago and London: University of Chicago Press.
— 1998. *The Last Dinosaur Book: The Life and Times of a Cultural Icon*. Chicago and London: University of Chicago Press.
— 1994. *Picture Theory*. Chicago and London: University of Chicago Press.
— ed. 1992. *Art and the Public Sphere*. Chicago and London: University of Chicago Press.
— 1986. *Iconology: Image, Text, Ideology*. Chicago: University of Chicago Press.
— ed. 1980. *The Language of Images*. Chicago: University of Chicago Press.
Mitchell, W. J. T. and Mark B. N. Hansen, eds. 2010. *Critical Terms for Media Studies*. Chicago and London: University of Chicago Press.
Mouffe, Chantal. 2005. *On the Political*. New York and London: Routledge.
Nanay, Bence. 2014. *Aesthetics as Philosophy of Perception*. Oxford: Oxford University Press.
— 2013. *Between Perception and Action*. Oxford: Oxford University Press.
— 2012a. "The Macro and the Micro: Andreas Gursky's Aesthetics." *Journal of Aesthetics and Art Criticism* 70: 91-100.
— 2012b "Anti-pornography: André Kertész's *Distortions*." In: *Art and Pornography*, edited by H. Maes and J. Levinson, 191-205. Oxford: Oxford University Press.
— 2011. "Perceiving Pictures." *Phenomenology and the Cognitive Sciences* 10: 461-480.
— 2010. "Inflected and Uninflected Perception of Pictures." In: *Philosophical Perspectives on Depiction*, edited by C. Abell and K. Bantilaki, 181-207. Oxford: Oxford University Press.

— 2009. "Narrative Pictures." *Journal of Aesthetics and Art Criticism* 67: 119-129.

— 2008. "Picture Perception and the Two Visual Subsystems." In: *Proceedings of the 30th Annual Conference of the Cognitive Science Society (CogSci 2008)*, edited by B. C. Love, K. McRae and V. M. Sloutsky, 975-980. Hillsdale, NJ: Lawrence Erlbaum.

— 2005. "Is Twofoldness Necessary for Representational Seeing?" *British Journal of Aesthetics* 45: 263-272.

— 2004. "Taking Twofoldness Seriously: Walton on Imagination and Depiction." *Journal of Aesthetics and Art Criticism* 62: 285-289.

Nelsen, Roger B. 2000. *Proofs without words II: More exercises in visual thinking*. The Mathematical Association of America.

— 1997. *Proofs without words: Exercises in visual thinking*. The Mathematical Association of America.

Nicholls, Andrea, and John M. Kennedy 1992. "Drawing Development: From Similarity of Features to Direction." *Child Development* 63(1): 227-241.

Podro, Michael. 1998. *Depiction*. New Haven: Yale University Press.

Rancière, Jacques. 1999. *Disagreement: Politics and Philosophy*, translated by J. Rose Minneapolis: University of Minnesota Press.

Reinhardt, Mark, Holly Edwards, and Erina Duganne, eds. 2007. *Beautiful Suffering: Photography and the Traffic in Pain*. Chicago: University of Chicago Press.

Roncero, Carlos, John M. Kennedy, and Ron Smyth. 2006. "Similes on the Internet Have Explanations." *Psychonomic Bulletin and Review* 13(1): 74-77.

Sartre, Jean-Paul. 2004. *The Imaginary: A Phenomenological Psychology of the Imagination*. Translated by J. Webber. London: Routledge.

Saussure, Ferdinand de. 1959. *Course in General Linguistics*. New York: Philosophical Library.

Silverman, Kaja. 1996. *The Threshold of the Visible World*. New York: Routledge.

Sparagana, John, and Mieke Bal. 2008. *Sleeping Beauty: A One-Artist Dictionary*. Chicago: University of Chicago Press.

Stafford, Barbara Maria. 2011. *A Field Guide to a New Meta-field:*

Bridging the Humanities-Neurosciences Divide. Chicago: University of Chicago Press.

— 2007. *Echo Objects: The Cognitive Work of Images*. Chicago: University of Chicago Press.

— 2001. *Devices of Wonder: From the World in a Box to Images on a Screen*. Los Angeles: Getty Publications.

— 1999. *Visual Analogy: Consciousness as the Art of Connecting*. Cambridge, Mass: MIT Press.

— 1994. *Artful Science: Enlightenment Entertainment and the Eclipse of Visual Education*. Cambridge, Mass.: MIT Press.

— 1991. *Body Criticism: Imaging the Unseen in Enlightenment Art and Medicine*. Cambridge, Mass.: MIT Press.

— 1984. *Voyage into Substance: Art, Science and the Illustrated Travel Account, 1760-1840*. Cambridge, Mass.: MIT Press.

— 1979. *Symbol and Myth: Humbert de Superville's Essay on Absolute Signs in Art*. Cranbury: University of Delaware.

Stoichita, Victor. 1999. *L'instauration du tableau: métapeinture à l'aube des temps modernes*, Geneva: Droz.

Thürlemann, Felix. 1982. *Paul Klee: analyse sémiotique de trois peintures*, Lausanne: L'Age d'Homme.

— 1979. "Die Farbe in der Malerei: symbolischer und semi-symbolischer Bedeutungsmodus." In: *Semiotics Unfolding: Proceedings of the Second Congress of the International Association for Semiotic Studies*, vol, 3, edited by Tasso Borbé,1389-1396. Vienna-Den Haag: Mouton.

— 1983. "The Function of Admiration in the Esthetic of the XVIIth Century." In: *Paris School Semiotics*, vol. II. edited by A.J. Greimas et al., 43-65. Toronto, Victoria University: Practice (= Toronto Semiotic Circle Monographs 4).

— 1985. "Le mode de signification 'immédiat' ou physionomique." In: *Exigences et perspectives de la sémiotique: recueil d'hommages pour A.J. Greimas*, edited by H. Parret and H.-G. Ruprecht, vol. II, 661-669. Amsterdam: John Benjamins.

— 1986. *Kandinsky* über *Kandinsky: der Künstler als Interpret eigener Werke*. Bern: Benteli.

— 1989. "Fictionality in Mantegna's San Zeno Altarpiece: Structures of Mimesis and the History of Painting." *New Literary History* 20, 747-761.

Kendall L. Walton

— 1990. *Vom Bild zum Raum: Beiträge zu einer semiotischen Kunstwissenschaft*. Cologne: DuMont.

— 2002. *Robert Campin. A Monograph with Critical Catalogue*. Munich/New York: Prestel.

— (with Steffen Bogen). 2003. "Jenseits der Opposition von Text und Bild: Überlegungen zu einer Theorie des Diagramms und des Diagrammatischen." In: *Die Bildwelt der Diagramme Joachims von Fiore: zur Medialität religiöspolitischer Programme im Mittelalter*, edited by Alexander Patschovsky, Stuttgart: Thorbecke, 1-22.

— 2004. "Vom Einzelbild zum ,hyperimage': eine neue Herausforderung für die kunstgeschichtliche Hermeneutik." In: *Les herméneutiques au seuil du XXIème siècle – évolution et débat actuel*, edited by Ada Neschke-Hentschke, Leuwen/Paris, 223-247.

— 2005. "Bild gegen Bild: für eine Theorie des vergleichenden Sehens." In: *Zwischen Literatur und Anthropologie – Diskurse, Medien, Performanzen*, edited by Aleida Assmann, Ulrich Gaier und Gisela Trommsdorff, Tübingen, 163-174.

— 2009. (With Steffen Bogen) *Rom. Eine Stadt in Karten von der Antike bis heute*, Primus Verlag, Darmstadt 2009.

— (with David Ganz) (eds.). 2010. *Das Bild im Plural: mehrteilige Bildformen zwischen Mittelalter und Gegenwart*. Berlin: Reimer.

— 2011. "The Paradoxical Rhetoric of Tears: Looking at the Madrid *Descent from the Cross*." In: *Crying in the Middle Ages: Tears of History*, editetd by Elina Gertsman, New York/London: Routledge.

Tufte, Edward. 2001. *The Visual Display of Quantitative Information*. Cheshire. Graphics Press.

— 1990. *Envisioning Information*. Cheshire: Graphics Press.

Walton, Kendall. 2012. "Fotografische Bilder." In: *Fotografie zwischen Dokumentation und Inszenierung*, edited by. J. Nida-Rümelin and J. Steinbrenner. Stuttgart: Hatje-Cantz.

— 2008. *Marvelous Images: On Values and the Arts*. New York and Oxford: Oxford University Press.

— 2008. "Experiencing Still Photographs: What Do You See and How Long Do You See It?" In: *Marvelous Images: On Values and the Arts*, 157-92. New York and Oxford: Oxford University Press.

— 1990. *Mimesis as Make-Believe: On the Foundations of the Representational Arts*. Cambridge, Mass.: Harvard University Press.

— 1984. "Transparent Pictures: On the Nature of Photographic Realism." Critical Inquiry, 11(2): 246-277.

— 1973. "Pictures as Make-Believe." *The Philosophical Review* 82(3): 283-319.

Willats, John. 2005. *Making Sense of Children's Drawings*. Mahwah: Lawrence Erlbaum.

— 1997. *Art and Representation: New Principles in the Analysis of Pictures*. Princeton: Princeton University Press.

Wittgenstein, Ludwig. 1998. *Culture and Value: Revised Edition*. Oxford: Blackwell.

Wnuczko, Marta, and John M. Kennedy. 2014. "Pointing to Azimuths and Elevations of Targets: Blind and Blindfolded-Sighted." *Perception* 43(2-3): 117-228.

Wollheim, Richard. 1980. *Art and its Objects*. Cambridge: Cambridge University Press.

— 1987. *Painting as an Art*. Princeton: Princeton University Press.

— 2003. "Richard Wollheim interviewed by John Rapko." San Francisco Art Institute, November 2003, https://www.academia.edu/4829390/Richard_Wollheim_interviewed_by

Wölfflin, Heinrich. 1964 [1888]. *Renaissance and Baroque*. Translated by K. Simon. London: Collins.

— 1952 [1899]. *Classic Art: An Introduction to the Italian Renaissance*. Translated by P. Murray and L. Murray. New York and London: Phaidon.

— 1932 [1915]. *Principles of Art*. Translated by M. D. Hottinger. New York: Dover.

www.ingramcontent.com/pod-product-compliance
Lightning Source LLC
Chambersburg PA
CBHW020421220526
45464CB00002B/513